# NOTARY PUBLIC
## JOURNAL

> *"The secret to success as a notary public is to be prepared, determined, and committed."*
>
> **GPL MOBILE NOTARY SERVICES**

© Copyright 2021

GPL Mobile Notary Services. All Rights Reserved.

*This book or any portion therof may not be reproduced, stored in any retrieval system, or transmitted in any form or by and means, electronic, mechanical, digital, photocopy, recording, or any other, without written permission from the publisher except brief quotations in printed reviews.*

Published By Boundless Butterfly Press LLC, New Jersey

ISBN: 978-1-956526-07-3

Printed in the United States of America

# Tips to Prepare for Your Notary Appointment

- ✓ Confirm appointment time with client
- ✓ Confirm client has required identification that is acceptable for your state guidelines
- ✓ Confirm the number of documents the client needs notarized
- ✓ Confirm if the notarization needs a witness and that all signers will be present
- ✓ Discuss any fees and method of payment prior to the appointment
- ✓ Verify you have your notary supplies required by your state guidelines

# Examples of Common Notary Supplies

- o Notary Stamp
- o Extra Pen
- o Notary Journal
- o Notary Ledger
- o Notary Bag

- ✓ Dress professionally – first impressions matter
- ✓ Arrive to the appointment earlier than scheduled
- ✓ Be focused and attentive to details
- ✓ Ask for a review – Good customer reviews will spread the word about your services.

**For more information about the author, notary tips, and other notary products please visit:**

www.gplmobilenotary.com

| \multicolumn{2}{c}{**NOTARY PUBLIC PERSONAL INFORMATION**} |
|---|---|
| Name: | |
| Address: | |
| Email: | |
| Phone: | |
| Fax: | |

## NOTARY LOG

| Full Name | Phone Number: | Record Number: **1** |
|---|---|---|
| Email Address: | Signer's Signature: | $ Amount charged: |
| Address: | | Method of Payment: |
| | Gas & Mileage: | ☐ Cash  ☐ Credit  ☐ Check |

| Notary Service(s) Provided: | Identification: | ID Number: |
|---|---|---|
| ☐ Jurat | ☐ ID Card  ☐ Credible Witness | Issued By: |
| ☐ Oath/Affirmations | ☐ Passport  ☐ Known Personally | Date Issued:  Expiration Date: |
| ☐ Acknowledgment | ☐ Driver's License | |
| ☐ Other: | ☐ Other: | |

| Witness Full Name: | Phone Number: | |
|---|---|---|
| Email Address: | Witness Signature: | Thumbprint: |
| Address: | | |

| Document Type: | Date/Time Notarized: | Document Date: |
|---|---|---|
| Comments: | | |

## NOTARY LOG

| Full Name | Phone Number: | Record Number: **2** |
|---|---|---|
| Email Address: | Signer's Signature: | $ Amount charged: |
| Address: | | Method of Payment: |
| | Gas & Mileage: | ☐ Cash  ☐ Credit  ☐ Check |

| Notary Service(s) Provided: | Identification: | ID Number: |
|---|---|---|
| ☐ Jurat | ☐ ID Card  ☐ Credible Witness | Issued By: |
| ☐ Oath/Affirmations | ☐ Passport  ☐ Known Personally | Date Issued:  Expiration Date: |
| ☐ Acknowledgment | ☐ Driver's License | |
| ☐ Other: | ☐ Other: | |

| Witness Full Name: | Phone Number: | |
|---|---|---|
| Email Address: | Witness Signature: | Thumbprint: |
| Address: | | |

| Document Type: | Date/Time Notarized: | Document Date: |
|---|---|---|
| Comments: | | |

## NOTARY LOG

| | | |
|---|---|---|
| Full Name | Phone Number: | Record Number: **3** |
| Email Address: | Signer's Signature: | $ Amount charged: |
| Address: | | Method of Payment: |
| | Gas & Mileage: | ☐ Cash   ☐ Credit   ☐ Check |
| Notary Service(s) Provided: | Identification: | ID Number: |
| ☐ Jurat | ☐ ID Card   ☐ Credible Witness | Issued By: |
| ☐ Oath/Affirmations | ☐ Passport   ☐ Known Personally | Date Issued: | Expiration Date: |
| ☐ Acknowledgment | ☐ Driver's License | | |
| ☐ Other: | ☐ Other: | | |

Witness Full Name:   Phone Number:

Email Address:   Witness Signature:   Thumbprint:

Address:

Document Type:   Date/Time Notarized:   Document Date:

Comments:

## NOTARY LOG

| | | |
|---|---|---|
| Full Name | Phone Number: | Record Number: **4** |
| Email Address: | Signer's Signature: | $ Amount charged: |
| Address: | | Method of Payment: |
| | Gas & Mileage: | ☐ Cash   ☐ Credit   ☐ Check |
| Notary Service(s) Provided: | Identification: | ID Number: |
| ☐ Jurat | ☐ ID Card   ☐ Credible Witness | Issued By: |
| ☐ Oath/Affirmations | ☐ Passport   ☐ Known Personally | Date Issued: | Expiration Date: |
| ☐ Acknowledgment | ☐ Driver's License | | |
| ☐ Other: | ☐ Other: | | |

Witness Full Name:   Phone Number:

Email Address:   Witness Signature:   Thumbprint:

Address:

Document Type:   Date/Time Notarized:   Document Date:

Comments:

## NOTARY LOG

| | | |
|---|---|---|
| Full Name | Phone Number: | Record Number: **5** |
| Email Address: | Signer's Signature: | $ Amount charged: |
| Address: | | Method of Payment: |
| | Gas & Mileage: | ☐ Cash  ☐ Credit  ☐ Check |
| Notary Service(s) Provided: | Identification: | ID Number: |
| ☐ Jurat | ☐ ID Card   ☐ Credible Witness | Issued By: |
| ☐ Oath/Affirmations | ☐ Passport   ☐ Known Personally | Date Issued:  Expiration Date: |
| ☐ Acknowledgment | ☐ Driver's License | |
| ☐ Other: | ☐ Other: | |
| Witness Full Name: | Phone Number: | |
| Email Address: | Witness Signature: | Thumbprint: |
| Address: | | |
| Document Type: | Date/Time Notarized: | Document Date: |
| Comments: | | |

## NOTARY LOG

| | | |
|---|---|---|
| Full Name | Phone Number: | Record Number: **6** |
| Email Address: | Signer's Signature: | $ Amount charged: |
| Address: | | Method of Payment: |
| | Gas & Mileage: | ☐ Cash  ☐ Credit  ☐ Check |
| Notary Service(s) Provided: | Identification: | ID Number: |
| ☐ Jurat | ☐ ID Card   ☐ Credible Witness | Issued By: |
| ☐ Oath/Affirmations | ☐ Passport   ☐ Known Personally | Date Issued:  Expiration Date: |
| ☐ Acknowledgment | ☐ Driver's License | |
| ☐ Other: | ☐ Other: | |
| Witness Full Name: | Phone Number: | |
| Email Address: | Witness Signature: | Thumbprint: |
| Address: | | |
| Document Type: | Date/Time Notarized: | Document Date: |
| Comments: | | |

## NOTARY LOG

| Full Name | Phone Number: | Record Number: **7** |
|---|---|---|
| Email Address: | Signer's Signature: | $ Amount charged: |
| Address: | | Method of Payment: |
| | Gas & Mileage: | ☐ Cash  ☐ Credit  ☐ Check |

| Notary Service(s) Provided: | Identification: | ID Number: |
|---|---|---|
| ☐ Jurat | ☐ ID Card  ☐ Credible Witness | Issued By: |
| ☐ Oath/Affirmations | ☐ Passport  ☐ Known Personally | Date Issued: | Expiration Date: |
| ☐ Acknowledgment | ☐ Driver's License | | |
| ☐ Other: | ☐ Other: | | |

| Witness Full Name: | Phone Number: | |
|---|---|---|
| Email Address: | Witness Signature: | Thumbprint: |
| Address: | | |

| Document Type: | Date/Time Notarized: | Document Date: |
|---|---|---|
| Comments: | | |

## NOTARY LOG

| Full Name | Phone Number: | Record Number: **8** |
|---|---|---|
| Email Address: | Signer's Signature: | $ Amount charged: |
| Address: | | Method of Payment: |
| | Gas & Mileage: | ☐ Cash  ☐ Credit  ☐ Check |

| Notary Service(s) Provided: | Identification: | ID Number: |
|---|---|---|
| ☐ Jurat | ☐ ID Card  ☐ Credible Witness | Issued By: |
| ☐ Oath/Affirmations | ☐ Passport  ☐ Known Personally | Date Issued: | Expiration Date: |
| ☐ Acknowledgment | ☐ Driver's License | | |
| ☐ Other: | ☐ Other: | | |

| Witness Full Name: | Phone Number: | |
|---|---|---|
| Email Address: | Witness Signature: | Thumbprint: |
| Address: | | |

| Document Type: | Date/Time Notarized: | Document Date: |
|---|---|---|
| Comments: | | |

## NOTARY LOG

| Full Name | Phone Number: | Record Number: **9** |
|---|---|---|
| Email Address: | Signer's Signature: | $ Amount charged: |
| Address: | | Method of Payment: |
| | Gas & Mileage: | ☐ Cash  ☐ Credit  ☐ Check |

| Notary Service(s) Provided: | Identification: | | ID Number: | |
|---|---|---|---|---|
| ☐ Jurat | ☐ ID Card | ☐ Credible Witness | Issued By: | |
| ☐ Oath/Affirmations | ☐ Passport | ☐ Known Personally | Date Issued: | Expiration Date: |
| ☐ Acknowledgment | ☐ Driver's License | | | |
| ☐ Other: | ☐ Other: | | | |

| Witness Full Name: | Phone Number: | |
|---|---|---|
| Email Address: | Witness Signature: | Thumbprint: |
| Address: | | |

| Document Type: | Date/Time Notarized: | Document Date: |
|---|---|---|
| Comments: | | |

---

## NOTARY LOG

| Full Name | Phone Number: | Record Number: **10** |
|---|---|---|
| Email Address: | Signer's Signature: | $ Amount charged: |
| Address: | | Method of Payment: |
| | Gas & Mileage: | ☐ Cash  ☐ Credit  ☐ Check |

| Notary Service(s) Provided: | Identification: | | ID Number: | |
|---|---|---|---|---|
| ☐ Jurat | ☐ ID Card | ☐ Credible Witness | Issued By: | |
| ☐ Oath/Affirmations | ☐ Passport | ☐ Known Personally | Date Issued: | Expiration Date: |
| ☐ Acknowledgment | ☐ Driver's License | | | |
| ☐ Other: | ☐ Other: | | | |

| Witness Full Name: | Phone Number: | |
|---|---|---|
| Email Address: | Witness Signature: | Thumbprint: |
| Address: | | |

| Document Type: | Date/Time Notarized: | Document Date: |
|---|---|---|
| Comments: | | |

## NOTARY LOG

| | | |
|---|---|---|
| Full Name | Phone Number: | Record Number: **11** |
| Email Address: | Signer's Signature: | $ Amount charged: |
| Address: | | Method of Payment: |
| | Gas & Mileage: | ☐ Cash  ☐ Credit  ☐ Check |
| Notary Service(s) Provided: | Identification: | ID Number: |
| ☐ Jurat | ☐ ID Card  ☐ Credible Witness | Issued By: |
| ☐ Oath/Affirmations | ☐ Passport  ☐ Known Personally | Date Issued: | Expiration Date: |
| ☐ Acknowledgment | ☐ Driver's License | | |
| ☐ Other: | ☐ Other: | | |

Witness Full Name: | Phone Number:
Email Address: | Witness Signature: | Thumbprint:
Address: |

Document Type: | Date/Time Notarized: | Document Date:
Comments:

## NOTARY LOG

| | | |
|---|---|---|
| Full Name | Phone Number: | Record Number: **12** |
| Email Address: | Signer's Signature: | $ Amount charged: |
| Address: | | Method of Payment: |
| | Gas & Mileage: | ☐ Cash  ☐ Credit  ☐ Check |
| Notary Service(s) Provided: | Identification: | ID Number: |
| ☐ Jurat | ☐ ID Card  ☐ Credible Witness | Issued By: |
| ☐ Oath/Affirmations | ☐ Passport  ☐ Known Personally | Date Issued: | Expiration Date: |
| ☐ Acknowledgment | ☐ Driver's License | | |
| ☐ Other: | ☐ Other: | | |

Witness Full Name: | Phone Number:
Email Address: | Witness Signature: | Thumbprint:
Address: |

Document Type: | Date/Time Notarized: | Document Date:
Comments:

## NOTARY LOG

| Full Name | Phone Number: | Record Number: **13** |
|---|---|---|
| Email Address: | Signer's Signature: | $ Amount charged: |
| Address: | | Method of Payment: |
| | Gas & Mileage: | ☐ Cash   ☐ Credit   ☐ Check |

| Notary Service(s) Provided: | Identification: | ID Number: |
|---|---|---|
| ☐ Jurat | ☐ ID Card   ☐ Credible Witness | Issued By: |
| ☐ Oath/Affirmations | ☐ Passport   ☐ Known Personally | Date Issued:   Expiration Date: |
| ☐ Acknowledgment | ☐ Driver's License | |
| ☐ Other: | ☐ Other: | |

| Witness Full Name: | Phone Number: | |
|---|---|---|
| Email Address: | Witness Signature: | Thumbprint: |
| Address: | | |

| Document Type: | Date/Time Notarized: | Document Date: |
|---|---|---|
| Comments: | | |

## NOTARY LOG

| Full Name | Phone Number: | Record Number: **14** |
|---|---|---|
| Email Address: | Signer's Signature: | $ Amount charged: |
| Address: | | Method of Payment: |
| | Gas & Mileage: | ☐ Cash   ☐ Credit   ☐ Check |

| Notary Service(s) Provided: | Identification: | ID Number: |
|---|---|---|
| ☐ Jurat | ☐ ID Card   ☐ Credible Witness | Issued By: |
| ☐ Oath/Affirmations | ☐ Passport   ☐ Known Personally | Date Issued:   Expiration Date: |
| ☐ Acknowledgment | ☐ Driver's License | |
| ☐ Other: | ☐ Other: | |

| Witness Full Name: | Phone Number: | |
|---|---|---|
| Email Address: | Witness Signature: | Thumbprint: |
| Address: | | |

| Document Type: | Date/Time Notarized: | Document Date: |
|---|---|---|
| Comments: | | |

## NOTARY LOG

| | | |
|---|---|---|
| Full Name | Phone Number: | Record Number: **15** |
| Email Address: | Signer's Signature: | $ Amount charged: |
| Address: | | Method of Payment: |
| | Gas & Mileage: | ☐ Cash  ☐ Credit  ☐ Check |
| Notary Service(s) Provided: | Identification: | ID Number: |
| ☐ Jurat | ☐ ID Card    ☐ Credible Witness | Issued By: |
| ☐ Oath/Affirmations | ☐ Passport    ☐ Known Personally | Date Issued:    Expiration Date: |
| ☐ Acknowledgment | ☐ Driver's License | |
| ☐ Other: | ☐ Other: | |

| | | |
|---|---|---|
| Witness Full Name: | Phone Number: | |
| Email Address: | Witness Signature: | Thumbprint: |
| Address: | | |
| Document Type:    Date/Time Notarized: | Document Date: | |
| Comments: | | |

## NOTARY LOG

| | | |
|---|---|---|
| Full Name | Phone Number: | Record Number: **16** |
| Email Address: | Signer's Signature: | $ Amount charged: |
| Address: | | Method of Payment: |
| | Gas & Mileage: | ☐ Cash  ☐ Credit  ☐ Check |
| Notary Service(s) Provided: | Identification: | ID Number: |
| ☐ Jurat | ☐ ID Card    ☐ Credible Witness | Issued By: |
| ☐ Oath/Affirmations | ☐ Passport    ☐ Known Personally | Date Issued:    Expiration Date: |
| ☐ Acknowledgment | ☐ Driver's License | |
| ☐ Other: | ☐ Other: | |

| | | |
|---|---|---|
| Witness Full Name: | Phone Number: | |
| Email Address: | Witness Signature: | Thumbprint: |
| Address: | | |
| Document Type:    Date/Time Notarized: | Document Date: | |
| Comments: | | |

## NOTARY LOG

| Full Name | Phone Number: | Record Number: **17** |
|---|---|---|
| Email Address: | Signer's Signature: | $ Amount charged: |
| Address: | | Method of Payment: |
| | Gas & Mileage: | ☐ Cash   ☐ Credit   ☐ Check |

| Notary Service(s) Provided: | Identification: | ID Number: |
|---|---|---|
| ☐ Jurat | ☐ ID Card   ☐ Credible Witness | Issued By: |
| ☐ Oath/Affirmations | ☐ Passport   ☐ Known Personally | Date Issued:   Expiration Date: |
| ☐ Acknowledgment | ☐ Driver's License | |
| ☐ Other: | ☐ Other: | |

| Witness Full Name: | Phone Number: | |
|---|---|---|
| Email Address: | Witness Signature: | Thumbprint: |
| Address: | | |

| Document Type: | Date/Time Notarized: | Document Date: |
|---|---|---|
| Comments: | | |

## NOTARY LOG

| Full Name | Phone Number: | Record Number: **18** |
|---|---|---|
| Email Address: | Signer's Signature: | $ Amount charged: |
| Address: | | Method of Payment: |
| | Gas & Mileage: | ☐ Cash   ☐ Credit   ☐ Check |

| Notary Service(s) Provided: | Identification: | ID Number: |
|---|---|---|
| ☐ Jurat | ☐ ID Card   ☐ Credible Witness | Issued By: |
| ☐ Oath/Affirmations | ☐ Passport   ☐ Known Personally | Date Issued:   Expiration Date: |
| ☐ Acknowledgment | ☐ Driver's License | |
| ☐ Other: | ☐ Other: | |

| Witness Full Name: | Phone Number: | |
|---|---|---|
| Email Address: | Witness Signature: | Thumbprint: |
| Address: | | |

| Document Type: | Date/Time Notarized: | Document Date: |
|---|---|---|
| Comments: | | |

# NOTARY LOG

| Full Name | Phone Number: | Record Number: **19** |
|---|---|---|
| Email Address: | Signer's Signature: | $ Amount charged: |
| Address: | | Method of Payment: |
| | Gas & Mileage: | ☐ Cash   ☐ Credit   ☐ Check |

| Notary Service(s) Provided: | Identification: | ID Number: |
|---|---|---|
| ☐ Jurat | ☐ ID Card   ☐ Credible Witness | Issued By: |
| ☐ Oath/Affirmations | ☐ Passport   ☐ Known Personally | Date Issued: | Expiration Date: |
| ☐ Acknowledgment | ☐ Driver's License | | |
| ☐ Other: | ☐ Other: | | |

| Witness Full Name: | Phone Number: | |
|---|---|---|
| Email Address: | Witness Signature: | Thumbprint: |
| Address: | | |

| Document Type: | Date/Time Notarized: | Document Date: |
|---|---|---|
| Comments: | | |

# NOTARY LOG

| Full Name | Phone Number: | Record Number: **20** |
|---|---|---|
| Email Address: | Signer's Signature: | $ Amount charged: |
| Address: | | Method of Payment: |
| | Gas & Mileage: | ☐ Cash   ☐ Credit   ☐ Check |

| Notary Service(s) Provided: | Identification: | ID Number: |
|---|---|---|
| ☐ Jurat | ☐ ID Card   ☐ Credible Witness | Issued By: |
| ☐ Oath/Affirmations | ☐ Passport   ☐ Known Personally | Date Issued: | Expiration Date: |
| ☐ Acknowledgment | ☐ Driver's License | | |
| ☐ Other: | ☐ Other: | | |

| Witness Full Name: | Phone Number: | |
|---|---|---|
| Email Address: | Witness Signature: | Thumbprint: |
| Address: | | |

| Document Type: | Date/Time Notarized: | Document Date: |
|---|---|---|
| Comments: | | |

## NOTARY LOG

| | | |
|---|---|---|
| Full Name | Phone Number: | Record Number: **21** |
| Email Address: | Signer's Signature: | $ Amount charged: |
| Address: | | Method of Payment: |
| | Gas & Mileage: | ☐ Cash  ☐ Credit  ☐ Check |
| Notary Service(s) Provided: | Identification: | ID Number: |
| ☐ Jurat | ☐ ID Card   ☐ Credible Witness | Issued By: |
| ☐ Oath/Affirmations | ☐ Passport   ☐ Known Personally | Date Issued:  Expiration Date: |
| ☐ Acknowledgment | ☐ Driver's License | |
| ☐ Other: | ☐ Other: | |

| | | |
|---|---|---|
| Witness Full Name: | Phone Number: | |
| Email Address: | Witness Signature: | Thumbprint: |
| Address: | | |
| Document Type:  Date/Time Notarized: | Document Date: | |
| Comments: | | |

## NOTARY LOG

| | | |
|---|---|---|
| Full Name | Phone Number: | Record Number: **22** |
| Email Address: | Signer's Signature: | $ Amount charged: |
| Address: | | Method of Payment: |
| | Gas & Mileage: | ☐ Cash  ☐ Credit  ☐ Check |
| Notary Service(s) Provided: | Identification: | ID Number: |
| ☐ Jurat | ☐ ID Card   ☐ Credible Witness | Issued By: |
| ☐ Oath/Affirmations | ☐ Passport   ☐ Known Personally | Date Issued:  Expiration Date: |
| ☐ Acknowledgment | ☐ Driver's License | |
| ☐ Other: | ☐ Other: | |

| | | |
|---|---|---|
| Witness Full Name: | Phone Number: | |
| Email Address: | Witness Signature: | Thumbprint: |
| Address: | | |
| Document Type:  Date/Time Notarized: | Document Date: | |
| Comments: | | |

## NOTARY LOG

| | | |
|---|---|---|
| Full Name | Phone Number: | Record Number: **23** |
| Email Address: | Signer's Signature: | $ Amount charged: |
| Address: | | Method of Payment: |
| | Gas & Mileage: | ☐ Cash  ☐ Credit  ☐ Check |
| Notary Service(s) Provided: | Identification: | ID Number: |
| ☐ Jurat | ☐ ID Card  ☐ Credible Witness | Issued By: |
| ☐ Oath/Affirmations | ☐ Passport  ☐ Known Personally | Date Issued:  Expiration Date: |
| ☐ Acknowledgment | ☐ Driver's License | |
| ☐ Other: | ☐ Other: | |
| Witness Full Name: | Phone Number: | |
| Email Address: | Witness Signature: | Thumbprint: |
| Address: | | |
| Document Type: | Date/Time Notarized: | Document Date: |
| Comments: | | |

## NOTARY LOG

| | | |
|---|---|---|
| Full Name | Phone Number: | Record Number: **24** |
| Email Address: | Signer's Signature: | $ Amount charged: |
| Address: | | Method of Payment: |
| | Gas & Mileage: | ☐ Cash  ☐ Credit  ☐ Check |
| Notary Service(s) Provided: | Identification: | ID Number: |
| ☐ Jurat | ☐ ID Card  ☐ Credible Witness | Issued By: |
| ☐ Oath/Affirmations | ☐ Passport  ☐ Known Personally | Date Issued:  Expiration Date: |
| ☐ Acknowledgment | ☐ Driver's License | |
| ☐ Other: | ☐ Other: | |
| Witness Full Name: | Phone Number: | |
| Email Address: | Witness Signature: | Thumbprint: |
| Address: | | |
| Document Type: | Date/Time Notarized: | Document Date: |
| Comments: | | |

## NOTARY LOG

| Full Name | Phone Number: | Record Number: **25** |
|---|---|---|
| Email Address: | Signer's Signature: | $ Amount charged: |
| Address: | | Method of Payment: |
| | Gas & Mileage: | ☐ Cash  ☐ Credit  ☐ Check |
| Notary Service(s) Provided: | Identification: | ID Number: |
| ☐ Jurat | ☐ ID Card  ☐ Credible Witness | Issued By: |
| ☐ Oath/Affirmations | ☐ Passport  ☐ Known Personally | Date Issued: / Expiration Date: |
| ☐ Acknowledgment | ☐ Driver's License | |
| ☐ Other: | ☐ Other: | |
| Witness Full Name: | | Phone Number: | |
| Email Address: | | Witness Signature: | Thumbprint: |
| Address: | | | |
| Document Type: | Date/Time Notarized: | Document Date: | |
| Comments: | | | |

## NOTARY LOG

| Full Name | Phone Number: | Record Number: **26** |
|---|---|---|
| Email Address: | Signer's Signature: | $ Amount charged: |
| Address: | | Method of Payment: |
| | Gas & Mileage: | ☐ Cash  ☐ Credit  ☐ Check |
| Notary Service(s) Provided: | Identification: | ID Number: |
| ☐ Jurat | ☐ ID Card  ☐ Credible Witness | Issued By: |
| ☐ Oath/Affirmations | ☐ Passport  ☐ Known Personally | Date Issued: / Expiration Date: |
| ☐ Acknowledgment | ☐ Driver's License | |
| ☐ Other: | ☐ Other: | |
| Witness Full Name: | | Phone Number: | |
| Email Address: | | Witness Signature: | Thumbprint: |
| Address: | | | |
| Document Type: | Date/Time Notarized: | Document Date: | |
| Comments: | | | |

# NOTARY LOG

| Full Name | Phone Number: | Record Number: **27** |
|---|---|---|
| Email Address: | Signer's Signature: | $ Amount charged: |
| Address: | | Method of Payment: |
| | Gas & Mileage: | ☐ Cash  ☐ Credit  ☐ Check |

| Notary Service(s) Provided: | Identification: | ID Number: |
|---|---|---|
| ☐ Jurat | ☐ ID Card   ☐ Credible Witness | Issued By: |
| ☐ Oath/Affirmations | ☐ Passport   ☐ Known Personally | Date Issued:  |  Expiration Date: |
| ☐ Acknowledgment | ☐ Driver's License | |
| ☐ Other: | ☐ Other: | |

| Witness Full Name: | Phone Number: | |
|---|---|---|
| Email Address: | Witness Signature: | Thumbprint: |
| Address: | | |

| Document Type: | Date/Time Notarized: | Document Date: |
|---|---|---|
| Comments: | | |

---

# NOTARY LOG

| Full Name | Phone Number: | Record Number: **28** |
|---|---|---|
| Email Address: | Signer's Signature: | $ Amount charged: |
| Address: | | Method of Payment: |
| | Gas & Mileage: | ☐ Cash  ☐ Credit  ☐ Check |

| Notary Service(s) Provided: | Identification: | ID Number: |
|---|---|---|
| ☐ Jurat | ☐ ID Card   ☐ Credible Witness | Issued By: |
| ☐ Oath/Affirmations | ☐ Passport   ☐ Known Personally | Date Issued:  |  Expiration Date: |
| ☐ Acknowledgment | ☐ Driver's License | |
| ☐ Other: | ☐ Other: | |

| Witness Full Name: | Phone Number: | |
|---|---|---|
| Email Address: | Witness Signature: | Thumbprint: |
| Address: | | |

| Document Type: | Date/Time Notarized: | Document Date: |
|---|---|---|
| Comments: | | |

## NOTARY LOG

| | | |
|---|---|---|
| Full Name | Phone Number: | Record Number: **29** |
| Email Address: | Signer's Signature: | $ Amount charged: |
| Address: | | Method of Payment: |
| | Gas & Mileage: | ☐ Cash  ☐ Credit  ☐ Check |
| Notary Service(s) Provided: | Identification: | ID Number: |
| ☐ Jurat | ☐ ID Card  ☐ Credible Witness | Issued By: |
| ☐ Oath/Affirmations | ☐ Passport  ☐ Known Personally | Date Issued:  Expiration Date: |
| ☐ Acknowledgment | ☐ Driver's License | |
| ☐ Other: | ☐ Other: | |
| Witness Full Name: | Phone Number: | |
| Email Address: | Witness Signature: | Thumbprint: |
| Address: | | |
| Document Type: | Date/Time Notarized:  Document Date: | |
| Comments: | | |

## NOTARY LOG

| | | |
|---|---|---|
| Full Name | Phone Number: | Record Number: **30** |
| Email Address: | Signer's Signature: | $ Amount charged: |
| Address: | | Method of Payment: |
| | Gas & Mileage: | ☐ Cash  ☐ Credit  ☐ Check |
| Notary Service(s) Provided: | Identification: | ID Number: |
| ☐ Jurat | ☐ ID Card  ☐ Credible Witness | Issued By: |
| ☐ Oath/Affirmations | ☐ Passport  ☐ Known Personally | Date Issued:  Expiration Date: |
| ☐ Acknowledgment | ☐ Driver's License | |
| ☐ Other: | ☐ Other: | |
| Witness Full Name: | Phone Number: | |
| Email Address: | Witness Signature: | Thumbprint: |
| Address: | | |
| Document Type: | Date/Time Notarized:  Document Date: | |
| Comments: | | |

## NOTARY LOG

| Full Name | Phone Number: | Record Number: **31** |
|---|---|---|
| Email Address: | Signer's Signature: | $ Amount charged: |
| Address: | | Method of Payment: |
| | Gas & Mileage: | ☐ Cash  ☐ Credit  ☐ Check |

| Notary Service(s) Provided: | Identification: | ID Number: |
|---|---|---|
| ☐ Jurat | ☐ ID Card  ☐ Credible Witness | Issued By: |
| ☐ Oath/Affirmations | ☐ Passport  ☐ Known Personally | Date Issued:  Expiration Date: |
| ☐ Acknowledgment | ☐ Driver's License | |
| ☐ Other: | ☐ Other: | |

| Witness Full Name: | Phone Number: | |
|---|---|---|
| Email Address: | Witness Signature: | Thumbprint: |
| Address: | | |

| Document Type: | Date/Time Notarized: | Document Date: |
|---|---|---|
| Comments: | | |

## NOTARY LOG

| Full Name | Phone Number: | Record Number: **32** |
|---|---|---|
| Email Address: | Signer's Signature: | $ Amount charged: |
| Address: | | Method of Payment: |
| | Gas & Mileage: | ☐ Cash  ☐ Credit  ☐ Check |

| Notary Service(s) Provided: | Identification: | ID Number: |
|---|---|---|
| ☐ Jurat | ☐ ID Card  ☐ Credible Witness | Issued By: |
| ☐ Oath/Affirmations | ☐ Passport  ☐ Known Personally | Date Issued:  Expiration Date: |
| ☐ Acknowledgment | ☐ Driver's License | |
| ☐ Other: | ☐ Other: | |

| Witness Full Name: | Phone Number: | |
|---|---|---|
| Email Address: | Witness Signature: | Thumbprint: |
| Address: | | |

| Document Type: | Date/Time Notarized: | Document Date: |
|---|---|---|
| Comments: | | |

## NOTARY LOG

| | | |
|---|---|---|
| Full Name | Phone Number: | Record Number: **33** |
| Email Address: | Signer's Signature: | $ Amount charged: |
| Address: | | Method of Payment: |
| | Gas & Mileage: | ☐ Cash ☐ Credit ☐ Check |
| Notary Service(s) Provided: | Identification: | ID Number: |
| ☐ Jurat | ☐ ID Card  ☐ Credible Witness | Issued By: |
| ☐ Oath/Affirmations | ☐ Passport  ☐ Known Personally | Date Issued: / Expiration Date: |
| ☐ Acknowledgment | ☐ Driver's License | |
| ☐ Other: | ☐ Other: | |
| Witness Full Name: | Phone Number: | |
| Email Address: | Witness Signature: | Thumbprint: |
| Address: | | |
| Document Type: | Date/Time Notarized: | Document Date: |
| Comments: | | |

## NOTARY LOG

| | | |
|---|---|---|
| Full Name | Phone Number: | Record Number: **34** |
| Email Address: | Signer's Signature: | $ Amount charged: |
| Address: | | Method of Payment: |
| | Gas & Mileage: | ☐ Cash ☐ Credit ☐ Check |
| Notary Service(s) Provided: | Identification: | ID Number: |
| ☐ Jurat | ☐ ID Card  ☐ Credible Witness | Issued By: |
| ☐ Oath/Affirmations | ☐ Passport  ☐ Known Personally | Date Issued: / Expiration Date: |
| ☐ Acknowledgment | ☐ Driver's License | |
| ☐ Other: | ☐ Other: | |
| Witness Full Name: | Phone Number: | |
| Email Address: | Witness Signature: | Thumbprint: |
| Address: | | |
| Document Type: | Date/Time Notarized: | Document Date: |
| Comments: | | |

## NOTARY LOG

| Full Name | Phone Number: | Record Number: **35** |
|---|---|---|
| Email Address: | Signer's Signature: | $ Amount charged: |
| Address: | | Method of Payment: |
| | Gas & Mileage: | ☐ Cash  ☐ Credit  ☐ Check |

| Notary Service(s) Provided: | Identification: | ID Number: |
|---|---|---|
| ☐ Jurat | ☐ ID Card  ☐ Credible Witness | Issued By: |
| ☐ Oath/Affirmations | ☐ Passport  ☐ Known Personally | Date Issued: | Expiration Date: |
| ☐ Acknowledgment | ☐ Driver's License | | |
| ☐ Other: | ☐ Other: | | |

| Witness Full Name: | Phone Number: | |
|---|---|---|
| Email Address: | Witness Signature: | Thumbprint: |
| Address: | | |

| Document Type: | Date/Time Notarized: | Document Date: |
|---|---|---|
| Comments: | | |

## NOTARY LOG

| Full Name | Phone Number: | Record Number: **36** |
|---|---|---|
| Email Address: | Signer's Signature: | $ Amount charged: |
| Address: | | Method of Payment: |
| | Gas & Mileage: | ☐ Cash  ☐ Credit  ☐ Check |

| Notary Service(s) Provided: | Identification: | ID Number: |
|---|---|---|
| ☐ Jurat | ☐ ID Card  ☐ Credible Witness | Issued By: |
| ☐ Oath/Affirmations | ☐ Passport  ☐ Known Personally | Date Issued: | Expiration Date: |
| ☐ Acknowledgment | ☐ Driver's License | | |
| ☐ Other: | ☐ Other: | | |

| Witness Full Name: | Phone Number: | |
|---|---|---|
| Email Address: | Witness Signature: | Thumbprint: |
| Address: | | |

| Document Type: | Date/Time Notarized: | Document Date: |
|---|---|---|
| Comments: | | |

## NOTARY LOG

| Full Name | Phone Number: | Record Number: **37** |
|---|---|---|
| Email Address: | Signer's Signature: | $ Amount charged: |
| Address: | | Method of Payment: |
| | Gas & Mileage: | ☐ Cash  ☐ Credit  ☐ Check |
| Notary Service(s) Provided: | Identification: | ID Number: |
| ☐ Jurat | ☐ ID Card   ☐ Credible Witness | Issued By: |
| ☐ Oath/Affirmations | ☐ Passport   ☐ Known Personally | Date Issued:  |  Expiration Date: |
| ☐ Acknowledgment | ☐ Driver's License | |
| ☐ Other: | ☐ Other: | |

| Witness Full Name: | Phone Number: | |
|---|---|---|
| Email Address: | Witness Signature: | Thumbprint: |
| Address: | | |

| Document Type: | Date/Time Notarized: | Document Date: |
|---|---|---|
| Comments: | | |

## NOTARY LOG

| Full Name | Phone Number: | Record Number: **38** |
|---|---|---|
| Email Address: | Signer's Signature: | $ Amount charged: |
| Address: | | Method of Payment: |
| | Gas & Mileage: | ☐ Cash  ☐ Credit  ☐ Check |
| Notary Service(s) Provided: | Identification: | ID Number: |
| ☐ Jurat | ☐ ID Card   ☐ Credible Witness | Issued By: |
| ☐ Oath/Affirmations | ☐ Passport   ☐ Known Personally | Date Issued:  |  Expiration Date: |
| ☐ Acknowledgment | ☐ Driver's License | |
| ☐ Other: | ☐ Other: | |

| Witness Full Name: | Phone Number: | |
|---|---|---|
| Email Address: | Witness Signature: | Thumbprint: |
| Address: | | |

| Document Type: | Date/Time Notarized: | Document Date: |
|---|---|---|
| Comments: | | |

## NOTARY LOG

| | | |
|---|---|---|
| Full Name | Phone Number: | Record Number: **39** |
| Email Address: | Signer's Signature: | $ Amount charged: |
| Address: | | Method of Payment: |
| | Gas & Mileage: | ☐ Cash   ☐ Credit   ☐ Check |
| Notary Service(s) Provided: | Identification: | ID Number: |
| ☐ Jurat | ☐ ID Card   ☐ Credible Witness | Issued By: |
| ☐ Oath/Affirmations | ☐ Passport   ☐ Known Personally | Date Issued: | Expiration Date: |
| ☐ Acknowledgment | ☐ Driver's License | | |
| ☐ Other: | ☐ Other: | | |

| | | |
|---|---|---|
| Witness Full Name: | Phone Number: | |
| Email Address: | Witness Signature: | Thumbprint: |
| Address: | | |
| Document Type: | Date/Time Notarized: | Document Date: |
| Comments: | | |

## NOTARY LOG

| | | |
|---|---|---|
| Full Name | Phone Number: | Record Number: **40** |
| Email Address: | Signer's Signature: | $ Amount charged: |
| Address: | | Method of Payment: |
| | Gas & Mileage: | ☐ Cash   ☐ Credit   ☐ Check |
| Notary Service(s) Provided: | Identification: | ID Number: |
| ☐ Jurat | ☐ ID Card   ☐ Credible Witness | Issued By: |
| ☐ Oath/Affirmations | ☐ Passport   ☐ Known Personally | Date Issued: | Expiration Date: |
| ☐ Acknowledgment | ☐ Driver's License | | |
| ☐ Other: | ☐ Other: | | |

| | | |
|---|---|---|
| Witness Full Name: | Phone Number: | |
| Email Address: | Witness Signature: | Thumbprint: |
| Address: | | |
| Document Type: | Date/Time Notarized: | Document Date: |
| Comments: | | |

# NOTARY LOG

| Full Name | Phone Number: | Record Number: **41** |
|---|---|---|
| Email Address: | Signer's Signature: | $ Amount charged: |
| Address: | | Method of Payment: |
| | Gas & Mileage: | ☐ Cash  ☐ Credit  ☐ Check |

| Notary Service(s) Provided: | Identification: | | ID Number: | |
|---|---|---|---|---|
| ☐ Jurat | ☐ ID Card | ☐ Credible Witness | Issued By: | |
| ☐ Oath/Affirmations | ☐ Passport | ☐ Known Personally | Date Issued: | Expiration Date: |
| ☐ Acknowledgment | ☐ Driver's License | | | |
| ☐ Other: | ☐ Other: | | | |

| Witness Full Name: | Phone Number: | |
|---|---|---|
| Email Address: | Witness Signature: | Thumbprint: |
| Address: | | |

| Document Type: | Date/Time Notarized: | Document Date: |
|---|---|---|
| Comments: | | |

# NOTARY LOG

| Full Name | Phone Number: | Record Number: **42** |
|---|---|---|
| Email Address: | Signer's Signature: | $ Amount charged: |
| Address: | | Method of Payment: |
| | Gas & Mileage: | ☐ Cash  ☐ Credit  ☐ Check |

| Notary Service(s) Provided: | Identification: | | ID Number: | |
|---|---|---|---|---|
| ☐ Jurat | ☐ ID Card | ☐ Credible Witness | Issued By: | |
| ☐ Oath/Affirmations | ☐ Passport | ☐ Known Personally | Date Issued: | Expiration Date: |
| ☐ Acknowledgment | ☐ Driver's License | | | |
| ☐ Other: | ☐ Other: | | | |

| Witness Full Name: | Phone Number: | |
|---|---|---|
| Email Address: | Witness Signature: | Thumbprint: |
| Address: | | |

| Document Type: | Date/Time Notarized: | Document Date: |
|---|---|---|
| Comments: | | |

## NOTARY LOG

| | | |
|---|---|---|
| Full Name | Phone Number: | Record Number: **43** |
| Email Address: | Signer's Signature: | $ Amount charged: |
| Address: | | Method of Payment: |
| | Gas & Mileage: | ☐ Cash  ☐ Credit  ☐ Check |

| Notary Service(s) Provided: | Identification: | | ID Number: | |
|---|---|---|---|---|
| ☐ Jurat | ☐ ID Card | ☐ Credible Witness | Issued By: | |
| ☐ Oath/Affirmations | ☐ Passport | ☐ Known Personally | Date Issued: | Expiration Date: |
| ☐ Acknowledgment | ☐ Driver's License | | | |
| ☐ Other: | ☐ Other: | | | |

| | | |
|---|---|---|
| Witness Full Name: | Phone Number: | |
| Email Address: | Witness Signature: | Thumbprint: |
| Address: | | |

| | | |
|---|---|---|
| Document Type: | Date/Time Notarized: | Document Date: |
| Comments: | | |

---

## NOTARY LOG

| | | |
|---|---|---|
| Full Name | Phone Number: | Record Number: **44** |
| Email Address: | Signer's Signature: | $ Amount charged: |
| Address: | | Method of Payment: |
| | Gas & Mileage: | ☐ Cash  ☐ Credit  ☐ Check |

| Notary Service(s) Provided: | Identification: | | ID Number: | |
|---|---|---|---|---|
| ☐ Jurat | ☐ ID Card | ☐ Credible Witness | Issued By: | |
| ☐ Oath/Affirmations | ☐ Passport | ☐ Known Personally | Date Issued: | Expiration Date: |
| ☐ Acknowledgment | ☐ Driver's License | | | |
| ☐ Other: | ☐ Other: | | | |

| | | |
|---|---|---|
| Witness Full Name: | Phone Number: | |
| Email Address: | Witness Signature: | Thumbprint: |
| Address: | | |

| | | |
|---|---|---|
| Document Type: | Date/Time Notarized: | Document Date: |
| Comments: | | |

## NOTARY LOG

| Full Name | Phone Number: | Record Number: **45** |
|---|---|---|
| Email Address: | Signer's Signature: | $ Amount charged: |
| Address: | | Method of Payment: |
| | Gas & Mileage: | ☐ Cash   ☐ Credit   ☐ Check |

| Notary Service(s) Provided: | Identification: | ID Number: |
|---|---|---|
| ☐ Jurat | ☐ ID Card    ☐ Credible Witness | Issued By: |
| ☐ Oath/Affirmations | ☐ Passport    ☐ Known Personally | Date Issued:    Expiration Date: |
| ☐ Acknowledgment | ☐ Driver's License | |
| ☐ Other: | ☐ Other: | |

| Witness Full Name: | Phone Number: | |
|---|---|---|
| Email Address: | Witness Signature: | Thumbprint: |
| Address: | | |

| Document Type: | Date/Time Notarized: | Document Date: |
|---|---|---|
| Comments: | | |

## NOTARY LOG

| Full Name | Phone Number: | Record Number: **46** |
|---|---|---|
| Email Address: | Signer's Signature: | $ Amount charged: |
| Address: | | Method of Payment: |
| | Gas & Mileage: | ☐ Cash   ☐ Credit   ☐ Check |

| Notary Service(s) Provided: | Identification: | ID Number: |
|---|---|---|
| ☐ Jurat | ☐ ID Card    ☐ Credible Witness | Issued By: |
| ☐ Oath/Affirmations | ☐ Passport    ☐ Known Personally | Date Issued:    Expiration Date: |
| ☐ Acknowledgment | ☐ Driver's License | |
| ☐ Other: | ☐ Other: | |

| Witness Full Name: | Phone Number: | |
|---|---|---|
| Email Address: | Witness Signature: | Thumbprint: |
| Address: | | |

| Document Type: | Date/Time Notarized: | Document Date: |
|---|---|---|
| Comments: | | |

## NOTARY LOG

| | | |
|---|---|---|
| Full Name | Phone Number: | Record Number: **47** |
| Email Address: | Signer's Signature: | $ Amount charged: |
| Address: | | Method of Payment: |
| | Gas & Mileage: | ☐ Cash  ☐ Credit  ☐ Check |
| Notary Service(s) Provided: | Identification: | ID Number: |
| ☐ Jurat | ☐ ID Card  ☐ Credible Witness | Issued By: |
| ☐ Oath/Affirmations | ☐ Passport  ☐ Known Personally | Date Issued:  Expiration Date: |
| ☐ Acknowledgment | ☐ Driver's License | |
| ☐ Other: | ☐ Other: | |
| Witness Full Name: | Phone Number: | |
| Email Address: | Witness Signature: | Thumbprint: |
| Address: | | |
| Document Type: | Date/Time Notarized: | Document Date: |
| Comments: | | |

## NOTARY LOG

| | | |
|---|---|---|
| Full Name | Phone Number: | Record Number: **48** |
| Email Address: | Signer's Signature: | $ Amount charged: |
| Address: | | Method of Payment: |
| | Gas & Mileage: | ☐ Cash  ☐ Credit  ☐ Check |
| Notary Service(s) Provided: | Identification: | ID Number: |
| ☐ Jurat | ☐ ID Card  ☐ Credible Witness | Issued By: |
| ☐ Oath/Affirmations | ☐ Passport  ☐ Known Personally | Date Issued:  Expiration Date: |
| ☐ Acknowledgment | ☐ Driver's License | |
| ☐ Other: | ☐ Other: | |
| Witness Full Name: | Phone Number: | |
| Email Address: | Witness Signature: | Thumbprint: |
| Address: | | |
| Document Type: | Date/Time Notarized: | Document Date: |
| Comments: | | |

## NOTARY LOG

| Full Name | Phone Number: | Record Number: **49** |
|---|---|---|
| Email Address: | Signer's Signature: | $ Amount charged: |
| Address: | | Method of Payment: |
| | Gas & Mileage: | ☐ Cash ☐ Credit ☐ Check |

| Notary Service(s) Provided: | Identification: | ID Number: |
|---|---|---|
| ☐ Jurat | ☐ ID Card ☐ Credible Witness | Issued By: |
| ☐ Oath/Affirmations | ☐ Passport ☐ Known Personally | Date Issued: / Expiration Date: |
| ☐ Acknowledgment | ☐ Driver's License | |
| ☐ Other: | ☐ Other: | |

| Witness Full Name: | Phone Number: | |
|---|---|---|
| Email Address: | Witness Signature: | Thumbprint: |
| Address: | | |

| Document Type: | Date/Time Notarized: | Document Date: |
|---|---|---|
| Comments: | | |

## NOTARY LOG

| Full Name | Phone Number: | Record Number: **50** |
|---|---|---|
| Email Address: | Signer's Signature: | $ Amount charged: |
| Address: | | Method of Payment: |
| | Gas & Mileage: | ☐ Cash ☐ Credit ☐ Check |

| Notary Service(s) Provided: | Identification: | ID Number: |
|---|---|---|
| ☐ Jurat | ☐ ID Card ☐ Credible Witness | Issued By: |
| ☐ Oath/Affirmations | ☐ Passport ☐ Known Personally | Date Issued: / Expiration Date: |
| ☐ Acknowledgment | ☐ Driver's License | |
| ☐ Other: | ☐ Other: | |

| Witness Full Name: | Phone Number: | |
|---|---|---|
| Email Address: | Witness Signature: | Thumbprint: |
| Address: | | |

| Document Type: | Date/Time Notarized: | Document Date: |
|---|---|---|
| Comments: | | |

## NOTARY LOG

| Full Name | Phone Number: | Record Number: **51** |
|---|---|---|
| Email Address: | Signer's Signature: | $ Amount charged: |
| Address: | | Method of Payment: |
| | Gas & Mileage: | ☐ Cash   ☐ Credit   ☐ Check |
| Notary Service(s) Provided: | Identification: | ID Number: |
| ☐ Jurat | ☐ ID Card   ☐ Credible Witness | Issued By: |
| ☐ Oath/Affirmations | ☐ Passport   ☐ Known Personally | Date Issued: | Expiration Date: |
| ☐ Acknowledgment | ☐ Driver's License | | |
| ☐ Other: | ☐ Other: | | |

| Witness Full Name: | Phone Number: | |
|---|---|---|
| Email Address: | Witness Signature: | Thumbprint: |
| Address: | | |

| Document Type: | Date/Time Notarized: | Document Date: |
|---|---|---|
| Comments: | | |

## NOTARY LOG

| Full Name | Phone Number: | Record Number: **52** |
|---|---|---|
| Email Address: | Signer's Signature: | $ Amount charged: |
| Address: | | Method of Payment: |
| | Gas & Mileage: | ☐ Cash   ☐ Credit   ☐ Check |
| Notary Service(s) Provided: | Identification: | ID Number: |
| ☐ Jurat | ☐ ID Card   ☐ Credible Witness | Issued By: |
| ☐ Oath/Affirmations | ☐ Passport   ☐ Known Personally | Date Issued: | Expiration Date: |
| ☐ Acknowledgment | ☐ Driver's License | | |
| ☐ Other: | ☐ Other: | | |

| Witness Full Name: | Phone Number: | |
|---|---|---|
| Email Address: | Witness Signature: | Thumbprint: |
| Address: | | |

| Document Type: | Date/Time Notarized: | Document Date: |
|---|---|---|
| Comments: | | |

## NOTARY LOG

| | | |
|---|---|---|
| Full Name | Phone Number: | Record Number: **53** |
| Email Address: | Signer's Signature: | $ Amount charged: |
| Address: | | Method of Payment: |
| | Gas & Mileage: | ☐ Cash ☐ Credit ☐ Check |
| Notary Service(s) Provided: | Identification: | ID Number: |
| ☐ Jurat | ☐ ID Card ☐ Credible Witness | Issued By: |
| ☐ Oath/Affirmations | ☐ Passport ☐ Known Personally | Date Issued: / Expiration Date: |
| ☐ Acknowledgment | ☐ Driver's License | |
| ☐ Other: | ☐ Other: | |
| Witness Full Name: | Phone Number: | |
| Email Address: | Witness Signature: | Thumbprint |
| Address: | | |
| Document Type: / Date/Time Notarized: | Document Date: | |
| Comments: | | |

## NOTARY LOG

| | | |
|---|---|---|
| Full Name | Phone Number: | Record Number: **54** |
| Email Address: | Signer's Signature: | $ Amount charged: |
| Address: | | Method of Payment: |
| | Gas & Mileage: | ☐ Cash ☐ Credit ☐ Check |
| Notary Service(s) Provided: | Identification: | ID Number: |
| ☐ Jurat | ☐ ID Card ☐ Credible Witness | Issued By: |
| ☐ Oath/Affirmations | ☐ Passport ☐ Known Personally | Date Issued: / Expiration Date: |
| ☐ Acknowledgment | ☐ Driver's License | |
| ☐ Other: | ☐ Other: | |
| Witness Full Name: | Phone Number: | |
| Email Address: | Witness Signature: | Thumbprint |
| Address: | | |
| Document Type: / Date/Time Notarized: | Document Date: | |
| Comments: | | |

## NOTARY LOG

| Full Name | Phone Number: | Record Number: **55** |
|---|---|---|
| Email Address: | Signer's Signature: | $ Amount charged: |
| Address: | | Method of Payment: |
| | Gas & Mileage: | ☐ Cash  ☐ Credit  ☐ Check |

| Notary Service(s) Provided: | Identification: | ID Number: |
|---|---|---|
| ☐ Jurat | ☐ ID Card   ☐ Credible Witness | Issued By: |
| ☐ Oath/Affirmations | ☐ Passport   ☐ Known Personally | Date Issued:   Expiration Date: |
| ☐ Acknowledgment | ☐ Driver's License | |
| ☐ Other: | ☐ Other: | |

Witness Full Name:    Phone Number:

| Email Address: | Witness Signature: | Thumbprint: |
|---|---|---|
| Address: | | |

| Document Type: | Date/Time Notarized: | Document Date: |
|---|---|---|

Comments:

---

## NOTARY LOG

| Full Name | Phone Number: | Record Number: **56** |
|---|---|---|
| Email Address: | Signer's Signature: | $ Amount charged: |
| Address: | | Method of Payment: |
| | Gas & Mileage: | ☐ Cash  ☐ Credit  ☐ Check |

| Notary Service(s) Provided: | Identification: | ID Number: |
|---|---|---|
| ☐ Jurat | ☐ ID Card   ☐ Credible Witness | Issued By: |
| ☐ Oath/Affirmations | ☐ Passport   ☐ Known Personally | Date Issued:   Expiration Date: |
| ☐ Acknowledgment | ☐ Driver's License | |
| ☐ Other: | ☐ Other: | |

Witness Full Name:    Phone Number:

| Email Address: | Witness Signature: | Thumbprint: |
|---|---|---|
| Address: | | |

| Document Type: | Date/Time Notarized: | Document Date: |
|---|---|---|

Comments:

## NOTARY LOG

| Full Name | Phone Number: | Record Number: **57** |
|---|---|---|
| Email Address: | Signer's Signature: | $ Amount charged: |
| Address: | | Method of Payment: |
| | Gas & Mileage: | ☐ Cash   ☐ Credit   ☐ Check |
| Notary Service(s) Provided: | Identification: | ID Number: |
| ☐ Jurat | ☐ ID Card   ☐ Credible Witness | Issued By: |
| ☐ Oath/Affirmations | ☐ Passport   ☐ Known Personally | Date Issued: | Expiration Date: |
| ☐ Acknowledgment | ☐ Driver's License | | |
| ☐ Other: | ☐ Other: | | |

| Witness Full Name: | Phone Number: | |
|---|---|---|
| Email Address: | Witness Signature: | Thumbprint: |
| Address: | | |

| Document Type: | Date/Time Notarized: | Document Date: |
|---|---|---|
| Comments: | | |

## NOTARY LOG

| Full Name | Phone Number: | Record Number: **58** |
|---|---|---|
| Email Address: | Signer's Signature: | $ Amount charged: |
| Address: | | Method of Payment: |
| | Gas & Mileage: | ☐ Cash   ☐ Credit   ☐ Check |
| Notary Service(s) Provided: | Identification: | ID Number: |
| ☐ Jurat | ☐ ID Card   ☐ Credible Witness | Issued By: |
| ☐ Oath/Affirmations | ☐ Passport   ☐ Known Personally | Date Issued: | Expiration Date: |
| ☐ Acknowledgment | ☐ Driver's License | | |
| ☐ Other: | ☐ Other: | | |

| Witness Full Name: | Phone Number: | |
|---|---|---|
| Email Address: | Witness Signature: | Thumbprint: |
| Address: | | |

| Document Type: | Date/Time Notarized: | Document Date: |
|---|---|---|
| Comments: | | |

# NOTARY LOG

| Full Name | Phone Number: | Record Number: **59** |
|---|---|---|
| Email Address: | Signer's Signature: | $ Amount charged: |
| Address: | | Method of Payment: |
| | Gas & Mileage: | ☐ Cash  ☐ Credit  ☐ Check |

| Notary Service(s) Provided: | Identification: | ID Number: |
|---|---|---|
| ☐ Jurat | ☐ ID Card   ☐ Credible Witness | Issued By: |
| ☐ Oath/Affirmations | ☐ Passport   ☐ Known Personally | Date Issued:   Expiration Date: |
| ☐ Acknowledgment | ☐ Driver's License | |
| ☐ Other: | ☐ Other: | |

| Witness Full Name: | Phone Number: | |
|---|---|---|
| Email Address: | Witness Signature: | Thumbprint: |
| Address: | | |

| Document Type: | Date/Time Notarized: | Document Date: |
|---|---|---|

Comments:

---

# NOTARY LOG

| Full Name | Phone Number: | Record Number: **60** |
|---|---|---|
| Email Address: | Signer's Signature: | $ Amount charged: |
| Address: | | Method of Payment: |
| | Gas & Mileage: | ☐ Cash  ☐ Credit  ☐ Check |

| Notary Service(s) Provided: | Identification: | ID Number: |
|---|---|---|
| ☐ Jurat | ☐ ID Card   ☐ Credible Witness | Issued By: |
| ☐ Oath/Affirmations | ☐ Passport   ☐ Known Personally | Date Issued:   Expiration Date: |
| ☐ Acknowledgment | ☐ Driver's License | |
| ☐ Other: | ☐ Other: | |

| Witness Full Name: | Phone Number: | |
|---|---|---|
| Email Address: | Witness Signature: | Thumbprint: |
| Address: | | |

| Document Type: | Date/Time Notarized: | Document Date: |
|---|---|---|

Comments:

## NOTARY LOG

| Full Name | Phone Number: | Record Number: **61** |
|---|---|---|
| Email Address: | Signer's Signature: | $ Amount charged: |
| Address: | | Method of Payment: |
| | Gas & Mileage: | ☐ Cash ☐ Credit ☐ Check |
| Notary Service(s) Provided: | Identification: | ID Number: |
| ☐ Jurat | ☐ ID Card ☐ Credible Witness | Issued By: |
| ☐ Oath/Affirmations | ☐ Passport ☐ Known Personally | Date Issued: / Expiration Date: |
| ☐ Acknowledgment | ☐ Driver's License | |
| ☐ Other: | ☐ Other: | |
| Witness Full Name: | Phone Number: | |
| Email Address: | Witness Signature: | Thumbprint: |
| Address: | | |
| Document Type: / Date/Time Notarized: | Document Date: | |
| Comments: | | |

## NOTARY LOG

| Full Name | Phone Number: | Record Number: **62** |
|---|---|---|
| Email Address: | Signer's Signature: | $ Amount charged: |
| Address: | | Method of Payment: |
| | Gas & Mileage: | ☐ Cash ☐ Credit ☐ Check |
| Notary Service(s) Provided: | Identification: | ID Number: |
| ☐ Jurat | ☐ ID Card ☐ Credible Witness | Issued By: |
| ☐ Oath/Affirmations | ☐ Passport ☐ Known Personally | Date Issued: / Expiration Date: |
| ☐ Acknowledgment | ☐ Driver's License | |
| ☐ Other: | ☐ Other: | |
| Witness Full Name: | Phone Number: | |
| Email Address: | Witness Signature: | Thumbprint: |
| Address: | | |
| Document Type: / Date/Time Notarized: | Document Date: | |
| Comments: | | |

## NOTARY LOG

| | | |
|---|---|---|
| Full Name | Phone Number: | Record Number: **63** |
| Email Address: | Signer's Signature: | $ Amount charged: |
| Address: | | Method of Payment: |
| | Gas & Mileage: | ☐ Cash   ☐ Credit   ☐ Check |
| Notary Service(s) Provided: | Identification: | ID Number: |
| ☐ Jurat | ☐ ID Card   ☐ Credible Witness | Issued By: |
| ☐ Oath/Affirmations | ☐ Passport   ☐ Known Personally | Date Issued: | Expiration Date: |
| ☐ Acknowledgment | ☐ Driver's License | | |
| ☐ Other: | ☐ Other: | | |

Witness Full Name: | Phone Number:
Email Address: | Witness Signature: | Thumbprint:
Address: | |
Document Type: | Date/Time Notarized: | Document Date:
Comments:

## NOTARY LOG

| | | |
|---|---|---|
| Full Name | Phone Number: | Record Number: **64** |
| Email Address: | Signer's Signature: | $ Amount charged: |
| Address: | | Method of Payment: |
| | Gas & Mileage: | ☐ Cash   ☐ Credit   ☐ Check |
| Notary Service(s) Provided: | Identification: | ID Number: |
| ☐ Jurat | ☐ ID Card   ☐ Credible Witness | Issued By: |
| ☐ Oath/Affirmations | ☐ Passport   ☐ Known Personally | Date Issued: | Expiration Date: |
| ☐ Acknowledgment | ☐ Driver's License | | |
| ☐ Other: | ☐ Other: | | |

Witness Full Name: | Phone Number:
Email Address: | Witness Signature: | Thumbprint:
Address: | |
Document Type: | Date/Time Notarized: | Document Date:
Comments:

## NOTARY LOG

| Full Name | Phone Number: | Record Number: **65** |
|---|---|---|
| Email Address: | Signer's Signature: | $ Amount charged: |
| Address: | | Method of Payment: |
| | Gas & Mileage: | ☐ Cash  ☐ Credit  ☐ Check |
| Notary Service(s) Provided: | Identification: | ID Number: |
| ☐ Jurat | ☐ ID Card  ☐ Credible Witness | Issued By: |
| ☐ Oath/Affirmations | ☐ Passport  ☐ Known Personally | Date Issued:  Expiration Date: |
| ☐ Acknowledgment | ☐ Driver's License | |
| ☐ Other: | ☐ Other: | |

| Witness Full Name: | Phone Number: | |
|---|---|---|
| Email Address: | Witness Signature: | Thumbprint: |
| Address: | | |

| Document Type: | Date/Time Notarized: | Document Date: |
|---|---|---|
| Comments: | | |

## NOTARY LOG

| Full Name | Phone Number: | Record Number: **66** |
|---|---|---|
| Email Address: | Signer's Signature: | $ Amount charged: |
| Address: | | Method of Payment: |
| | Gas & Mileage: | ☐ Cash  ☐ Credit  ☐ Check |
| Notary Service(s) Provided: | Identification: | ID Number: |
| ☐ Jurat | ☐ ID Card  ☐ Credible Witness | Issued By: |
| ☐ Oath/Affirmations | ☐ Passport  ☐ Known Personally | Date Issued:  Expiration Date: |
| ☐ Acknowledgment | ☐ Driver's License | |
| ☐ Other: | ☐ Other: | |

| Witness Full Name: | Phone Number: | |
|---|---|---|
| Email Address: | Witness Signature: | Thumbprint: |
| Address: | | |

| Document Type: | Date/Time Notarized: | Document Date: |
|---|---|---|
| Comments: | | |

## NOTARY LOG

| Full Name | Phone Number: | Record Number: **67** |
|---|---|---|
| Email Address: | Signer's Signature: | $ Amount charged: |
| Address: | | Method of Payment: |
| | Gas & Mileage: | ☐ Cash  ☐ Credit  ☐ Check |

| Notary Service(s) Provided: | Identification: | ID Number: |
|---|---|---|
| ☐ Jurat | ☐ ID Card   ☐ Credible Witness | Issued By: |
| ☐ Oath/Affirmations | ☐ Passport   ☐ Known Personally | Date Issued:   Expiration Date: |
| ☐ Acknowledgment | ☐ Driver's License | |
| ☐ Other: | ☐ Other: | |

| Witness Full Name: | Phone Number: | |
|---|---|---|
| Email Address: | Witness Signature: | Thumbprint: |
| Address: | | |

| Document Type: | Date/Time Notarized: | Document Date: |
|---|---|---|

Comments:

---

## NOTARY LOG

| Full Name | Phone Number: | Record Number: **68** |
|---|---|---|
| Email Address: | Signer's Signature: | $ Amount charged: |
| Address: | | Method of Payment: |
| | Gas & Mileage: | ☐ Cash  ☐ Credit  ☐ Check |

| Notary Service(s) Provided: | Identification: | ID Number: |
|---|---|---|
| ☐ Jurat | ☐ ID Card   ☐ Credible Witness | Issued By: |
| ☐ Oath/Affirmations | ☐ Passport   ☐ Known Personally | Date Issued:   Expiration Date: |
| ☐ Acknowledgment | ☐ Driver's License | |
| ☐ Other: | ☐ Other: | |

| Witness Full Name: | Phone Number: | |
|---|---|---|
| Email Address: | Witness Signature: | Thumbprint: |
| Address: | | |

| Document Type: | Date/Time Notarized: | Document Date: |
|---|---|---|

Comments:

## NOTARY LOG

| Full Name | Phone Number: | Record Number: **69** |
|---|---|---|
| Email Address: | Signer's Signature: | $ Amount charged: |
| Address: | | Method of Payment: |
| | Gas & Mileage: | ☐ Cash   ☐ Credit   ☐ Check |

| Notary Service(s) Provided: | Identification: | ID Number: |
|---|---|---|
| ☐ Jurat | ☐ ID Card   ☐ Credible Witness | Issued By: |
| ☐ Oath/Affirmations | ☐ Passport   ☐ Known Personally | Date Issued:   Expiration Date: |
| ☐ Acknowledgment | ☐ Driver's License | |
| ☐ Other: | ☐ Other: | |

| Witness Full Name: | Phone Number: | |
|---|---|---|
| Email Address: | Witness Signature: | Thumbprint: |
| Address: | | |

| Document Type: | Date/Time Notarized: | Document Date: |
|---|---|---|
| Comments: | | |

## NOTARY LOG

| Full Name | Phone Number: | Record Number: **70** |
|---|---|---|
| Email Address: | Signer's Signature: | $ Amount charged: |
| Address: | | Method of Payment: |
| | Gas & Mileage: | ☐ Cash   ☐ Credit   ☐ Check |

| Notary Service(s) Provided: | Identification: | ID Number: |
|---|---|---|
| ☐ Jurat | ☐ ID Card   ☐ Credible Witness | Issued By: |
| ☐ Oath/Affirmations | ☐ Passport   ☐ Known Personally | Date Issued:   Expiration Date: |
| ☐ Acknowledgment | ☐ Driver's License | |
| ☐ Other: | ☐ Other: | |

| Witness Full Name: | Phone Number: | |
|---|---|---|
| Email Address: | Witness Signature: | Thumbprint: |
| Address: | | |

| Document Type: | Date/Time Notarized: | Document Date: |
|---|---|---|
| Comments: | | |

## NOTARY LOG

| Full Name | Phone Number: | Record Number: **71** |
|---|---|---|
| Email Address: | Signer's Signature: | $ Amount charged: |
| Address: | | Method of Payment: |
| | Gas & Mileage: | ☐ Cash  ☐ Credit  ☐ Check |

| Notary Service(s) Provided: | Identification: | ID Number: |
|---|---|---|
| ☐ Jurat | ☐ ID Card   ☐ Credible Witness | Issued By: |
| ☐ Oath/Affirmations | ☐ Passport   ☐ Known Personally | Date Issued:   Expiration Date: |
| ☐ Acknowledgment | ☐ Driver's License | |
| ☐ Other: | ☐ Other: | |

| Witness Full Name: | Phone Number: | |
|---|---|---|
| Email Address: | Witness Signature: | Thumbprint: |
| Address: | | |

| Document Type: | Date/Time Notarized: | Document Date: |
|---|---|---|
| Comments: | | |

## NOTARY LOG

| Full Name | Phone Number: | Record Number: **72** |
|---|---|---|
| Email Address: | Signer's Signature: | $ Amount charged: |
| Address: | | Method of Payment: |
| | Gas & Mileage: | ☐ Cash  ☐ Credit  ☐ Check |

| Notary Service(s) Provided: | Identification: | ID Number: |
|---|---|---|
| ☐ Jurat | ☐ ID Card   ☐ Credible Witness | Issued By: |
| ☐ Oath/Affirmations | ☐ Passport   ☐ Known Personally | Date Issued:   Expiration Date: |
| ☐ Acknowledgment | ☐ Driver's License | |
| ☐ Other: | ☐ Other: | |

| Witness Full Name: | Phone Number: | |
|---|---|---|
| Email Address: | Witness Signature: | Thumbprint: |
| Address: | | |

| Document Type: | Date/Time Notarized: | Document Date: |
|---|---|---|
| Comments: | | |

## NOTARY LOG

| Full Name | Phone Number: | Record Number: **73** |
|---|---|---|
| Email Address: | Signer's Signature: | $ Amount charged: |
| Address: | | Method of Payment: |
| | Gas & Mileage: | ☐ Cash   ☐ Credit   ☐ Check |

| Notary Service(s) Provided: | Identification: | ID Number: |
|---|---|---|
| ☐ Jurat | ☐ ID Card   ☐ Credible Witness | Issued By: |
| ☐ Oath/Affirmations | ☐ Passport   ☐ Known Personally | Date Issued:   Expiration Date: |
| ☐ Acknowledgment | ☐ Driver's License | |
| ☐ Other: | ☐ Other: | |

| Witness Full Name: | Phone Number: | |
|---|---|---|
| Email Address: | Witness Signature: | Thumbprint: |
| Address: | | |

| Document Type: | Date/Time Notarized: | Document Date: |
|---|---|---|
| Comments: | | |

## NOTARY LOG

| Full Name | Phone Number: | Record Number: **74** |
|---|---|---|
| Email Address: | Signer's Signature: | $ Amount charged: |
| Address: | | Method of Payment: |
| | Gas & Mileage: | ☐ Cash   ☐ Credit   ☐ Check |

| Notary Service(s) Provided: | Identification: | ID Number: |
|---|---|---|
| ☐ Jurat | ☐ ID Card   ☐ Credible Witness | Issued By: |
| ☐ Oath/Affirmations | ☐ Passport   ☐ Known Personally | Date Issued:   Expiration Date: |
| ☐ Acknowledgment | ☐ Driver's License | |
| ☐ Other: | ☐ Other: | |

| Witness Full Name: | Phone Number: | |
|---|---|---|
| Email Address: | Witness Signature: | Thumbprint: |
| Address: | | |

| Document Type: | Date/Time Notarized: | Document Date: |
|---|---|---|
| Comments: | | |

## NOTARY LOG

| Full Name | Phone Number: | Record Number: **75** |
|---|---|---|
| Email Address: | Signer's Signature: | $ Amount charged: |
| Address: | | Method of Payment: |
| | Gas & Mileage: | ☐ Cash    ☐ Credit    ☐ Check |

| Notary Service(s) Provided: | Identification: | ID Number: |
|---|---|---|
| ☐ Jurat | ☐ ID Card    ☐ Credible Witness | Issued By: |
| ☐ Oath/Affirmations | ☐ Passport    ☐ Known Personally | Date Issued:    Expiration Date: |
| ☐ Acknowledgment | ☐ Driver's License | |
| ☐ Other: | ☐ Other: | |

| Witness Full Name: | Phone Number: | |
|---|---|---|
| Email Address: | Witness Signature: | Thumbprint: |
| Address: | | |

| Document Type: | Date/Time Notarized: | Document Date: |
|---|---|---|
| Comments: | | |

## NOTARY LOG

| Full Name | Phone Number: | Record Number: **76** |
|---|---|---|
| Email Address: | Signer's Signature: | $ Amount charged: |
| Address: | | Method of Payment: |
| | Gas & Mileage: | ☐ Cash    ☐ Credit    ☐ Check |

| Notary Service(s) Provided: | Identification: | ID Number: |
|---|---|---|
| ☐ Jurat | ☐ ID Card    ☐ Credible Witness | Issued By: |
| ☐ Oath/Affirmations | ☐ Passport    ☐ Known Personally | Date Issued:    Expiration Date: |
| ☐ Acknowledgment | ☐ Driver's License | |
| ☐ Other: | ☐ Other: | |

| Witness Full Name: | Phone Number: | |
|---|---|---|
| Email Address: | Witness Signature: | Thumbprint: |
| Address: | | |

| Document Type: | Date/Time Notarized: | Document Date: |
|---|---|---|
| Comments: | | |

## NOTARY LOG

| Full Name | Phone Number: | Record Number: **77** |
|---|---|---|
| Email Address: | Signer's Signature: | $ Amount charged: |
| Address: | | Method of Payment: |
| | Gas & Mileage: | ☐ Cash   ☐ Credit   ☐ Check |

| Notary Service(s) Provided: | Identification: | ID Number: |
|---|---|---|
| ☐ Jurat | ☐ ID Card   ☐ Credible Witness | Issued By: |
| ☐ Oath/Affirmations | ☐ Passport   ☐ Known Personally | Date Issued:   Expiration Date: |
| ☐ Acknowledgment | ☐ Driver's License | |
| ☐ Other: | ☐ Other: | |

| Witness Full Name: | Phone Number: | |
|---|---|---|
| Email Address: | Witness Signature: | Thumbprint: |
| Address: | | |

| Document Type: | Date/Time Notarized: | Document Date: |

Comments:

---

## NOTARY LOG

| Full Name | Phone Number: | Record Number: **78** |
|---|---|---|
| Email Address: | Signer's Signature: | $ Amount charged: |
| Address: | | Method of Payment: |
| | Gas & Mileage: | ☐ Cash   ☐ Credit   ☐ Check |

| Notary Service(s) Provided: | Identification: | ID Number: |
|---|---|---|
| ☐ Jurat | ☐ ID Card   ☐ Credible Witness | Issued By: |
| ☐ Oath/Affirmations | ☐ Passport   ☐ Known Personally | Date Issued:   Expiration Date: |
| ☐ Acknowledgment | ☐ Driver's License | |
| ☐ Other: | ☐ Other: | |

| Witness Full Name: | Phone Number: | |
|---|---|---|
| Email Address: | Witness Signature: | Thumbprint: |
| Address: | | |

| Document Type: | Date/Time Notarized: | Document Date: |

Comments:

## NOTARY LOG

| Full Name | Phone Number: | Record Number: **79** |
|---|---|---|
| Email Address: | Signer's Signature: | $ Amount charged: |
| Address: | | Method of Payment: |
| | Gas & Mileage: | ☐ Cash   ☐ Credit   ☐ Check |

| Notary Service(s) Provided: | Identification: | ID Number: |
|---|---|---|
| ☐ Jurat | ☐ ID Card   ☐ Credible Witness | Issued By: |
| ☐ Oath/Affirmations | ☐ Passport   ☐ Known Personally | Date Issued:   Expiration Date: |
| ☐ Acknowledgment | ☐ Driver's License | |
| ☐ Other: | ☐ Other: | |

| Witness Full Name: | Phone Number: | |
|---|---|---|
| Email Address: | Witness Signature: | Thumbprint: |
| Address: | | |

| Document Type: | Date/Time Notarized: | Document Date: |
|---|---|---|
| Comments: | | |

---

## NOTARY LOG

| Full Name | Phone Number: | Record Number: **80** |
|---|---|---|
| Email Address: | Signer's Signature: | $ Amount charged: |
| Address: | | Method of Payment: |
| | Gas & Mileage: | ☐ Cash   ☐ Credit   ☐ Check |

| Notary Service(s) Provided: | Identification: | ID Number: |
|---|---|---|
| ☐ Jurat | ☐ ID Card   ☐ Credible Witness | Issued By: |
| ☐ Oath/Affirmations | ☐ Passport   ☐ Known Personally | Date Issued:   Expiration Date: |
| ☐ Acknowledgment | ☐ Driver's License | |
| ☐ Other: | ☐ Other: | |

| Witness Full Name: | Phone Number: | |
|---|---|---|
| Email Address: | Witness Signature: | Thumbprint: |
| Address: | | |

| Document Type: | Date/Time Notarized: | Document Date: |
|---|---|---|
| Comments: | | |

## NOTARY LOG

| Full Name | Phone Number: | Record Number: **81** |
|---|---|---|
| Email Address: | Signer's Signature: | $ Amount charged: |
| Address: | | Method of Payment: |
| | Gas & Mileage: | ☐ Cash   ☐ Credit   ☐ Check |
| Notary Service(s) Provided: | Identification: | ID Number: |
| ☐ Jurat | ☐ ID Card   ☐ Credible Witness | Issued By: |
| ☐ Oath/Affirmations | ☐ Passport   ☐ Known Personally | Date Issued: | Expiration Date: |
| ☐ Acknowledgment | ☐ Driver's License | | |
| ☐ Other: | ☐ Other: | | |

| Witness Full Name: | Phone Number: | |
|---|---|---|
| Email Address: | Witness Signature: | Thumbprint: |
| Address: | | |

| Document Type: | Date/Time Notarized: | Document Date: | |
|---|---|---|---|
| Comments: | | | |

## NOTARY LOG

| Full Name | Phone Number: | Record Number: **82** |
|---|---|---|
| Email Address: | Signer's Signature: | $ Amount charged: |
| Address: | | Method of Payment: |
| | Gas & Mileage: | ☐ Cash   ☐ Credit   ☐ Check |
| Notary Service(s) Provided: | Identification: | ID Number: |
| ☐ Jurat | ☐ ID Card   ☐ Credible Witness | Issued By: |
| ☐ Oath/Affirmations | ☐ Passport   ☐ Known Personally | Date Issued: | Expiration Date: |
| ☐ Acknowledgment | ☐ Driver's License | | |
| ☐ Other: | ☐ Other: | | |

| Witness Full Name: | Phone Number: | |
|---|---|---|
| Email Address: | Witness Signature: | Thumbprint: |
| Address: | | |

| Document Type: | Date/Time Notarized: | Document Date: | |
|---|---|---|---|
| Comments: | | | |

## NOTARY LOG

| | | |
|---|---|---|
| Full Name | Phone Number: | Record Number: **83** |
| Email Address: | Signer's Signature: | $ Amount charged: |
| Address: | | Method of Payment: |
| | Gas & Mileage: | ☐ Cash   ☐ Credit   ☐ Check |
| Notary Service(s) Provided: | Identification: | ID Number: |
| ☐ Jurat | ☐ ID Card    ☐ Credible Witness | Issued By: |
| ☐ Oath/Affirmations | ☐ Passport    ☐ Known Personally | Date Issued:    Expiration Date: |
| ☐ Acknowledgment | ☐ Driver's License | |
| ☐ Other: | ☐ Other: | |
| Witness Full Name: | Phone Number: | |
| Email Address: | Witness Signature: | Thumbprint: |
| Address: | | |
| Document Type:    Date/Time Notarized: | Document Date: | |
| Comments: | | |

## NOTARY LOG

| | | |
|---|---|---|
| Full Name | Phone Number: | Record Number: **84** |
| Email Address: | Signer's Signature: | $ Amount charged: |
| Address: | | Method of Payment: |
| | Gas & Mileage: | ☐ Cash   ☐ Credit   ☐ Check |
| Notary Service(s) Provided: | Identification: | ID Number: |
| ☐ Jurat | ☐ ID Card    ☐ Credible Witness | Issued By: |
| ☐ Oath/Affirmations | ☐ Passport    ☐ Known Personally | Date Issued:    Expiration Date: |
| ☐ Acknowledgment | ☐ Driver's License | |
| ☐ Other: | ☐ Other: | |
| Witness Full Name: | Phone Number: | |
| Email Address: | Witness Signature: | Thumbprint: |
| Address: | | |
| Document Type:    Date/Time Notarized: | Document Date: | |
| Comments: | | |

## NOTARY LOG

| | | |
|---|---|---|
| Full Name | Phone Number: | Record Number: **85** |
| Email Address: | Signer's Signature: | $ Amount charged: |
| Address: | | Method of Payment: |
| | Gas & Mileage: | ☐ Cash   ☐ Credit   ☐ Check |
| Notary Service(s) Provided: | Identification: | ID Number: |
| ☐ Jurat | ☐ ID Card     ☐ Credible Witness | Issued By: |
| ☐ Oath/Affirmations | ☐ Passport    ☐ Known Personally | Date Issued:     Expiration Date: |
| ☐ Acknowledgment | ☐ Driver's License | |
| ☐ Other: | ☐ Other: | |
| Witness Full Name: | Phone Number: | |
| Email Address: | Witness Signature: | Thumbprint: |
| Address: | | |
| Document Type: | Date/Time Notarized: | Document Date: |
| Comments: | | |

## NOTARY LOG

| | | |
|---|---|---|
| Full Name | Phone Number: | Record Number: **86** |
| Email Address: | Signer's Signature: | $ Amount charged: |
| Address: | | Method of Payment: |
| | Gas & Mileage: | ☐ Cash   ☐ Credit   ☐ Check |
| Notary Service(s) Provided: | Identification: | ID Number: |
| ☐ Jurat | ☐ ID Card     ☐ Credible Witness | Issued By: |
| ☐ Oath/Affirmations | ☐ Passport    ☐ Known Personally | Date Issued:     Expiration Date: |
| ☐ Acknowledgment | ☐ Driver's License | |
| ☐ Other: | ☐ Other: | |
| Witness Full Name: | Phone Number: | |
| Email Address: | Witness Signature: | Thumbprint: |
| Address: | | |
| Document Type: | Date/Time Notarized: | Document Date: |
| Comments: | | |

## NOTARY LOG

| | | |
|---|---|---|
| Full Name | Phone Number: | Record Number: **87** |
| Email Address: | Signer's Signature: | $ Amount charged: |
| Address: | | Method of Payment: |
| | Gas & Mileage: | ☐ Cash ☐ Credit ☐ Check |
| Notary Service(s) Provided: | Identification: | ID Number: |
| ☐ Jurat | ☐ ID Card ☐ Credible Witness | Issued By: |
| ☐ Oath/Affirmations | ☐ Passport ☐ Known Personally | Date Issued: | Expiration Date: |
| ☐ Acknowledgment | ☐ Driver's License | |
| ☐ Other: | ☐ Other: | |

Witness Full Name: | Phone Number:
Email Address: | Witness Signature: | Thumbprint:
Address: |
Document Type: | Date/Time Notarized: | Document Date:
Comments:

## NOTARY LOG

| | | |
|---|---|---|
| Full Name | Phone Number: | Record Number: **88** |
| Email Address: | Signer's Signature: | $ Amount charged: |
| Address: | | Method of Payment: |
| | Gas & Mileage: | ☐ Cash ☐ Credit ☐ Check |
| Notary Service(s) Provided: | Identification: | ID Number: |
| ☐ Jurat | ☐ ID Card ☐ Credible Witness | Issued By: |
| ☐ Oath/Affirmations | ☐ Passport ☐ Known Personally | Date Issued: | Expiration Date: |
| ☐ Acknowledgment | ☐ Driver's License | |
| ☐ Other: | ☐ Other: | |

Witness Full Name: | Phone Number:
Email Address: | Witness Signature: | Thumbprint:
Address: |
Document Type: | Date/Time Notarized: | Document Date:
Comments:

# NOTARY LOG

| Full Name | Phone Number: | Record Number: **89** |
|---|---|---|
| Email Address: | Signer's Signature: | $ Amount charged: |
| Address: | | Method of Payment: |
| | Gas & Mileage: | ☐ Cash ☐ Credit ☐ Check |
| Notary Service(s) Provided: | Identification: | ID Number: |
| ☐ Jurat | ☐ ID Card ☐ Credible Witness | Issued By: |
| ☐ Oath/Affirmations | ☐ Passport ☐ Known Personally | Date Issued: / Expiration Date: |
| ☐ Acknowledgment | ☐ Driver's License | |
| ☐ Other: | ☐ Other: | |
| Witness Full Name: | Phone Number: | |
| Email Address: | Witness Signature: | Thumbprint: |
| Address: | | |
| Document Type: / Date/Time Notarized: | Document Date: | |
| Comments: | | |

# NOTARY LOG

| Full Name | Phone Number: | Record Number: **90** |
|---|---|---|
| Email Address: | Signer's Signature: | $ Amount charged: |
| Address: | | Method of Payment: |
| | Gas & Mileage: | ☐ Cash ☐ Credit ☐ Check |
| Notary Service(s) Provided: | Identification: | ID Number: |
| ☐ Jurat | ☐ ID Card ☐ Credible Witness | Issued By: |
| ☐ Oath/Affirmations | ☐ Passport ☐ Known Personally | Date Issued: / Expiration Date: |
| ☐ Acknowledgment | ☐ Driver's License | |
| ☐ Other: | ☐ Other: | |
| Witness Full Name: | Phone Number: | |
| Email Address: | Witness Signature: | Thumbprint: |
| Address: | | |
| Document Type: / Date/Time Notarized: | Document Date: | |
| Comments: | | |

# NOTARY LOG

| Full Name | Phone Number: | Record Number: **91** |
|---|---|---|
| Email Address: | Signer's Signature: | $ Amount charged: |
| Address: | | Method of Payment: |
| | Gas & Mileage: | ☐ Cash  ☐ Credit  ☐ Check |

| Notary Service(s) Provided: | Identification: | ID Number: |
|---|---|---|
| ☐ Jurat | ☐ ID Card  ☐ Credible Witness | Issued By: |
| ☐ Oath/Affirmations | ☐ Passport  ☐ Known Personally | Date Issued:  Expiration Date: |
| ☐ Acknowledgment | ☐ Driver's License | |
| ☐ Other: | ☐ Other: | |

Witness Full Name:     Phone Number:

Email Address:     Witness Signature:     Thumbprint:

Address:

Document Type:     Date/Time Notarized:     Document Date:

Comments:

---

# NOTARY LOG

| Full Name | Phone Number: | Record Number: **92** |
|---|---|---|
| Email Address: | Signer's Signature: | $ Amount charged: |
| Address: | | Method of Payment: |
| | Gas & Mileage: | ☐ Cash  ☐ Credit  ☐ Check |

| Notary Service(s) Provided: | Identification: | ID Number: |
|---|---|---|
| ☐ Jurat | ☐ ID Card  ☐ Credible Witness | Issued By: |
| ☐ Oath/Affirmations | ☐ Passport  ☐ Known Personally | Date Issued:  Expiration Date: |
| ☐ Acknowledgment | ☐ Driver's License | |
| ☐ Other: | ☐ Other: | |

Witness Full Name:     Phone Number:

Email Address:     Witness Signature:     Thumbprint:

Address:

Document Type:     Date/Time Notarized:     Document Date:

Comments:

## NOTARY LOG

| | | |
|---|---|---|
| Full Name | Phone Number: | Record Number: **93** |
| Email Address: | Signer's Signature: | $ Amount charged: |
| Address: | | Method of Payment: |
| | Gas & Mileage: | ☐ Cash  ☐ Credit  ☐ Check |

| Notary Service(s) Provided: | Identification: | ID Number: |
|---|---|---|
| ☐ Jurat | ☐ ID Card   ☐ Credible Witness | Issued By: |
| ☐ Oath/Affirmations | ☐ Passport  ☐ Known Personally | Date Issued:   Expiration Date: |
| ☐ Acknowledgment | ☐ Driver's License | |
| ☐ Other: | ☐ Other: | |

| | | |
|---|---|---|
| Witness Full Name: | Phone Number: | |
| Email Address: | Witness Signature: | Thumbprint: |
| Address: | | |
| Document Type: | Date/Time Notarized: | Document Date: |
| Comments: | | |

## NOTARY LOG

| | | |
|---|---|---|
| Full Name | Phone Number: | Record Number: **94** |
| Email Address: | Signer's Signature: | $ Amount charged: |
| Address: | | Method of Payment: |
| | Gas & Mileage: | ☐ Cash  ☐ Credit  ☐ Check |

| Notary Service(s) Provided: | Identification: | ID Number: |
|---|---|---|
| ☐ Jurat | ☐ ID Card   ☐ Credible Witness | Issued By: |
| ☐ Oath/Affirmations | ☐ Passport  ☐ Known Personally | Date Issued:   Expiration Date: |
| ☐ Acknowledgment | ☐ Driver's License | |
| ☐ Other: | ☐ Other: | |

| | | |
|---|---|---|
| Witness Full Name: | Phone Number: | |
| Email Address: | Witness Signature: | Thumbprint: |
| Address: | | |
| Document Type: | Date/Time Notarized: | Document Date: |
| Comments: | | |

## NOTARY LOG

| | | |
|---|---|---|
| Full Name | Phone Number: | Record Number: **95** |
| Email Address: | Signer's Signature: | $ Amount charged: |
| Address: | | Method of Payment: |
| | Gas & Mileage: | ☐ Cash  ☐ Credit  ☐ Check |
| Notary Service(s) Provided: | Identification: | ID Number: |
| ☐ Jurat | ☐ ID Card  ☐ Credible Witness | Issued By: |
| ☐ Oath/Affirmations | ☐ Passport  ☐ Known Personally | Date Issued:  Expiration Date: |
| ☐ Acknowledgment | ☐ Driver's License | |
| ☐ Other: | ☐ Other: | |

| | |
|---|---|
| Witness Full Name: | Phone Number: |
| Email Address: | Witness Signature:  Thumbprint: |
| Address: | |
| Document Type:  Date/Time Notarized: | Document Date: |
| Comments: | |

## NOTARY LOG

| | | |
|---|---|---|
| Full Name | Phone Number: | Record Number: **96** |
| Email Address: | Signer's Signature: | $ Amount charged: |
| Address: | | Method of Payment: |
| | Gas & Mileage: | ☐ Cash  ☐ Credit  ☐ Check |
| Notary Service(s) Provided: | Identification: | ID Number: |
| ☐ Jurat | ☐ ID Card  ☐ Credible Witness | Issued By: |
| ☐ Oath/Affirmations | ☐ Passport  ☐ Known Personally | Date Issued:  Expiration Date: |
| ☐ Acknowledgment | ☐ Driver's License | |
| ☐ Other: | ☐ Other: | |

| | |
|---|---|
| Witness Full Name: | Phone Number: |
| Email Address: | Witness Signature:  Thumbprint: |
| Address: | |
| Document Type:  Date/Time Notarized: | Document Date: |
| Comments: | |

## NOTARY LOG

| Full Name | Phone Number: | Record Number: **97** |
|---|---|---|
| Email Address: | Signer's Signature: | $ Amount charged: |
| Address: | | Method of Payment: |
| | Gas & Mileage: | ☐ Cash  ☐ Credit  ☐ Check |

| Notary Service(s) Provided: | Identification: | ID Number: |
|---|---|---|
| ☐ Jurat | ☐ ID Card   ☐ Credible Witness | Issued By: |
| ☐ Oath/Affirmations | ☐ Passport   ☐ Known Personally | Date Issued:   Expiration Date: |
| ☐ Acknowledgment | ☐ Driver's License | |
| ☐ Other: | ☐ Other: | |

| Witness Full Name: | Phone Number: | |
|---|---|---|
| Email Address: | Witness Signature: | Thumbprint: |
| Address: | | |

| Document Type: | Date/Time Notarized: | Document Date: |
|---|---|---|
| Comments: | | |

## NOTARY LOG

| Full Name | Phone Number: | Record Number: **98** |
|---|---|---|
| Email Address: | Signer's Signature: | $ Amount charged: |
| Address: | | Method of Payment: |
| | Gas & Mileage: | ☐ Cash  ☐ Credit  ☐ Check |

| Notary Service(s) Provided: | Identification: | ID Number: |
|---|---|---|
| ☐ Jurat | ☐ ID Card   ☐ Credible Witness | Issued By: |
| ☐ Oath/Affirmations | ☐ Passport   ☐ Known Personally | Date Issued:   Expiration Date: |
| ☐ Acknowledgment | ☐ Driver's License | |
| ☐ Other: | ☐ Other: | |

| Witness Full Name: | Phone Number: | |
|---|---|---|
| Email Address: | Witness Signature: | Thumbprint: |
| Address: | | |

| Document Type: | Date/Time Notarized: | Document Date: |
|---|---|---|
| Comments: | | |

## NOTARY LOG

| Full Name | Phone Number: | Record Number: **99** |
|---|---|---|
| Email Address: | Signer's Signature: | $ Amount charged: |
| Address: | | Method of Payment: |
| | Gas & Mileage: | ☐ Cash  ☐ Credit  ☐ Check |

| Notary Service(s) Provided: | Identification: | ID Number: |
|---|---|---|
| ☐ Jurat | ☐ ID Card    ☐ Credible Witness | Issued By: |
| ☐ Oath/Affirmations | ☐ Passport   ☐ Known Personally | Date Issued:   Expiration Date: |
| ☐ Acknowledgment | ☐ Driver's License | |
| ☐ Other: | ☐ Other: | |

| Witness Full Name: | Phone Number: | |
|---|---|---|
| Email Address: | Witness Signature: | Thumbprint: |
| Address: | | |

| Document Type: | Date/Time Notarized: | Document Date: |
|---|---|---|
| Comments: | | |

## NOTARY LOG

| Full Name | Phone Number: | Record Number: **100** |
|---|---|---|
| Email Address: | Signer's Signature: | $ Amount charged: |
| Address: | | Method of Payment: |
| | Gas & Mileage: | ☐ Cash  ☐ Credit  ☐ Check |

| Notary Service(s) Provided: | Identification: | ID Number: |
|---|---|---|
| ☐ Jurat | ☐ ID Card    ☐ Credible Witness | Issued By: |
| ☐ Oath/Affirmations | ☐ Passport   ☐ Known Personally | Date Issued:   Expiration Date: |
| ☐ Acknowledgment | ☐ Driver's License | |
| ☐ Other: | ☐ Other: | |

| Witness Full Name: | Phone Number: | |
|---|---|---|
| Email Address: | Witness Signature: | Thumbprint: |
| Address: | | |

| Document Type: | Date/Time Notarized: | Document Date: |
|---|---|---|
| Comments: | | |

## NOTARY LOG

| Full Name | Phone Number: | Record Number: **101** |
|---|---|---|
| Email Address: | Signer's Signature: | $ Amount charged: |
| Address: | | Method of Payment: |
| | Gas & Mileage: | ☐ Cash   ☐ Credit   ☐ Check |
| Notary Service(s) Provided: | Identification: | ID Number: |
| ☐ Jurat | ☐ ID Card   ☐ Credible Witness | Issued By: |
| ☐ Oath/Affirmations | ☐ Passport   ☐ Known Personally | Date Issued:   Expiration Date: |
| ☐ Acknowledgment | ☐ Driver's License | |
| ☐ Other: | ☐ Other: | |
| Witness Full Name: | | Phone Number: |
| Email Address: | Witness Signature: | Thumbprint: |
| Address: | | |
| Document Type: | Date/Time Notarized: | Document Date: |
| Comments: | | |

## NOTARY LOG

| Full Name | Phone Number: | Record Number: **102** |
|---|---|---|
| Email Address: | Signer's Signature: | $ Amount charged: |
| Address: | | Method of Payment: |
| | Gas & Mileage: | ☐ Cash   ☐ Credit   ☐ Check |
| Notary Service(s) Provided: | Identification: | ID Number: |
| ☐ Jurat | ☐ ID Card   ☐ Credible Witness | Issued By: |
| ☐ Oath/Affirmations | ☐ Passport   ☐ Known Personally | Date Issued:   Expiration Date: |
| ☐ Acknowledgment | ☐ Driver's License | |
| ☐ Other: | ☐ Other: | |
| Witness Full Name: | | Phone Number: |
| Email Address: | Witness Signature: | Thumbprint: |
| Address: | | |
| Document Type: | Date/Time Notarized: | Document Date: |
| Comments: | | |

## NOTARY LOG

| | | |
|---|---|---|
| Full Name | Phone Number: | Record Number: **103** |
| Email Address: | Signer's Signature: | $ Amount charged: |
| Address: | | Method of Payment: |
| | Gas & Mileage: | ☐ Cash   ☐ Credit   ☐ Check |
| Notary Service(s) Provided: | Identification: | ID Number: |
| ☐ Jurat | ☐ ID Card   ☐ Credible Witness | Issued By: |
| ☐ Oath/Affirmations | ☐ Passport   ☐ Known Personally | Date Issued:   Expiration Date: |
| ☐ Acknowledgment | ☐ Driver's License | |
| ☐ Other: | ☐ Other: | |

| | | |
|---|---|---|
| Witness Full Name: | | Phone Number: |
| Email Address: | Witness Signature: | Thumbprint: |
| Address: | | |
| Document Type: | Date/Time Notarized: | Document Date: |
| Comments: | | |

## NOTARY LOG

| | | |
|---|---|---|
| Full Name | Phone Number: | Record Number: **104** |
| Email Address: | Signer's Signature: | $ Amount charged: |
| Address: | | Method of Payment: |
| | Gas & Mileage: | ☐ Cash   ☐ Credit   ☐ Check |
| Notary Service(s) Provided: | Identification: | ID Number: |
| ☐ Jurat | ☐ ID Card   ☐ Credible Witness | Issued By: |
| ☐ Oath/Affirmations | ☐ Passport   ☐ Known Personally | Date Issued:   Expiration Date: |
| ☐ Acknowledgment | ☐ Driver's License | |
| ☐ Other: | ☐ Other: | |

| | | |
|---|---|---|
| Witness Full Name: | | Phone Number: |
| Email Address: | Witness Signature: | Thumbprint: |
| Address: | | |
| Document Type: | Date/Time Notarized: | Document Date: |
| Comments: | | |

## NOTARY LOG

| Full Name | Phone Number: | Record Number: **105** |
|---|---|---|
| Email Address: | Signer's Signature: | $ Amount charged: |
| Address: | | Method of Payment: |
| | Gas & Mileage: | ☐ Cash  ☐ Credit  ☐ Check |

| Notary Service(s) Provided: | Identification: | ID Number: |
|---|---|---|
| ☐ Jurat | ☐ ID Card   ☐ Credible Witness | Issued By: |
| ☐ Oath/Affirmations | ☐ Passport   ☐ Known Personally | Date Issued:   Expiration Date: |
| ☐ Acknowledgment | ☐ Driver's License | |
| ☐ Other: | ☐ Other: | |

| Witness Full Name: | Phone Number: | |
|---|---|---|
| Email Address: | Witness Signature: | Thumbprint: |
| Address: | | |

| Document Type: | Date/Time Notarized: | Document Date: |
|---|---|---|
| Comments: | | |

---

## NOTARY LOG

| Full Name | Phone Number: | Record Number: **106** |
|---|---|---|
| Email Address: | Signer's Signature: | $ Amount charged: |
| Address: | | Method of Payment: |
| | Gas & Mileage: | ☐ Cash  ☐ Credit  ☐ Check |

| Notary Service(s) Provided: | Identification: | ID Number: |
|---|---|---|
| ☐ Jurat | ☐ ID Card   ☐ Credible Witness | Issued By: |
| ☐ Oath/Affirmations | ☐ Passport   ☐ Known Personally | Date Issued:   Expiration Date: |
| ☐ Acknowledgment | ☐ Driver's License | |
| ☐ Other: | ☐ Other: | |

| Witness Full Name: | Phone Number: | |
|---|---|---|
| Email Address: | Witness Signature: | Thumbprint: |
| Address: | | |

| Document Type: | Date/Time Notarized: | Document Date: |
|---|---|---|
| Comments: | | |

## NOTARY LOG

| Full Name | Phone Number: | Record Number: **107** |
|---|---|---|
| Email Address: | Signer's Signature: | $ Amount charged: |
| Address: | | Method of Payment: |
| | Gas & Mileage: | ☐ Cash   ☐ Credit   ☐ Check |

| Notary Service(s) Provided: | Identification: | ID Number: |
|---|---|---|
| ☐ Jurat | ☐ ID Card   ☐ Credible Witness | Issued By: |
| ☐ Oath/Affirmations | ☐ Passport   ☐ Known Personally | Date Issued: | Expiration Date: |
| ☐ Acknowledgment | ☐ Driver's License | | |
| ☐ Other: | ☐ Other: | | |

| Witness Full Name: | Phone Number: | |
|---|---|---|
| Email Address: | Witness Signature: | Thumbprint: |
| Address: | | |

| Document Type: | Date/Time Notarized: | Document Date: |
|---|---|---|
| Comments: | | |

---

## NOTARY LOG

| Full Name | Phone Number: | Record Number: **108** |
|---|---|---|
| Email Address: | Signer's Signature: | $ Amount charged: |
| Address: | | Method of Payment: |
| | Gas & Mileage: | ☐ Cash   ☐ Credit   ☐ Check |

| Notary Service(s) Provided: | Identification: | ID Number: |
|---|---|---|
| ☐ Jurat | ☐ ID Card   ☐ Credible Witness | Issued By: |
| ☐ Oath/Affirmations | ☐ Passport   ☐ Known Personally | Date Issued: | Expiration Date: |
| ☐ Acknowledgment | ☐ Driver's License | | |
| ☐ Other: | ☐ Other: | | |

| Witness Full Name: | Phone Number: | |
|---|---|---|
| Email Address: | Witness Signature: | Thumbprint: |
| Address: | | |

| Document Type: | Date/Time Notarized: | Document Date: |
|---|---|---|
| Comments: | | |

## NOTARY LOG

| Full Name | Phone Number: | Record Number: **109** |
|---|---|---|
| Email Address: | Signer's Signature: | $ Amount charged: |
| Address: | | Method of Payment: |
| | Gas & Mileage: | ☐ Cash  ☐ Credit  ☐ Check |

| Notary Service(s) Provided: | Identification: | ID Number: |
|---|---|---|
| ☐ Jurat | ☐ ID Card  ☐ Credible Witness | Issued By: |
| ☐ Oath/Affirmations | ☐ Passport  ☐ Known Personally | Date Issued:  Expiration Date: |
| ☐ Acknowledgment | ☐ Driver's License | |
| ☐ Other: | ☐ Other: | |

| Witness Full Name: | Phone Number: | |
|---|---|---|
| Email Address: | Witness Signature: | Thumbprint: |
| Address: | | |

| Document Type: | Date/Time Notarized: | Document Date: |
|---|---|---|
| Comments: | | |

## NOTARY LOG

| Full Name | Phone Number: | Record Number: **110** |
|---|---|---|
| Email Address: | Signer's Signature: | $ Amount charged: |
| Address: | | Method of Payment: |
| | Gas & Mileage: | ☐ Cash  ☐ Credit  ☐ Check |

| Notary Service(s) Provided: | Identification: | ID Number: |
|---|---|---|
| ☐ Jurat | ☐ ID Card  ☐ Credible Witness | Issued By: |
| ☐ Oath/Affirmations | ☐ Passport  ☐ Known Personally | Date Issued:  Expiration Date: |
| ☐ Acknowledgment | ☐ Driver's License | |
| ☐ Other: | ☐ Other: | |

| Witness Full Name: | Phone Number: | |
|---|---|---|
| Email Address: | Witness Signature: | Thumbprint: |
| Address: | | |

| Document Type: | Date/Time Notarized: | Document Date: |
|---|---|---|
| Comments: | | |

## NOTARY LOG

| Full Name | Phone Number: | Record Number: **111** |
|---|---|---|
| Email Address: | Signer's Signature: | $ Amount charged: |
| Address: | | Method of Payment: |
| | Gas & Mileage: | ☐ Cash   ☐ Credit   ☐ Check |

| Notary Service(s) Provided: | Identification: | ID Number: |
|---|---|---|
| ☐ Jurat | ☐ ID Card   ☐ Credible Witness | Issued By: |
| ☐ Oath/Affirmations | ☐ Passport   ☐ Known Personally | Date Issued:   Expiration Date: |
| ☐ Acknowledgment | ☐ Driver's License | |
| ☐ Other: | ☐ Other: | |

| Witness Full Name: | Phone Number: | |
|---|---|---|
| Email Address: | Witness Signature: | Thumbprint: |
| Address: | | |

| Document Type: | Date/Time Notarized: | Document Date: |
|---|---|---|
| Comments: | | |

---

## NOTARY LOG

| Full Name | Phone Number: | Record Number: **112** |
|---|---|---|
| Email Address: | Signer's Signature: | $ Amount charged: |
| Address: | | Method of Payment: |
| | Gas & Mileage: | ☐ Cash   ☐ Credit   ☐ Check |

| Notary Service(s) Provided: | Identification: | ID Number: |
|---|---|---|
| ☐ Jurat | ☐ ID Card   ☐ Credible Witness | Issued By: |
| ☐ Oath/Affirmations | ☐ Passport   ☐ Known Personally | Date Issued:   Expiration Date: |
| ☐ Acknowledgment | ☐ Driver's License | |
| ☐ Other: | ☐ Other: | |

| Witness Full Name: | Phone Number: | |
|---|---|---|
| Email Address: | Witness Signature: | Thumbprint: |
| Address: | | |

| Document Type: | Date/Time Notarized: | Document Date: |
|---|---|---|
| Comments: | | |

## NOTARY LOG

| Full Name | Phone Number: | Record Number: **113** |
|---|---|---|
| Email Address: | Signer's Signature: | $ Amount charged: |
| Address: | | Method of Payment: |
| | Gas & Mileage: | ☐ Cash  ☐ Credit  ☐ Check |

Notary Service(s) Provided:

☐ Jurat

☐ Oath/Affirmations

☐ Acknowledgment

☐ Other:

Identification:

☐ ID Card    ☐ Credible Witness

☐ Passport    ☐ Known Personally

☐ Driver's License

☐ Other:

ID Number:

Issued By:

Date Issued:    Expiration Date:

Witness Full Name:    Phone Number:

Email Address:    Witness Signature:    Thumbprint:

Address:

Document Type:    Date/Time Notarized:    Document Date:

Comments:

---

## NOTARY LOG

| Full Name | Phone Number: | Record Number: **114** |
|---|---|---|
| Email Address: | Signer's Signature: | $ Amount charged: |
| Address: | | Method of Payment: |
| | Gas & Mileage: | ☐ Cash  ☐ Credit  ☐ Check |

Notary Service(s) Provided:

☐ Jurat

☐ Oath/Affirmations

☐ Acknowledgment

☐ Other:

Identification:

☐ ID Card    ☐ Credible Witness

☐ Passport    ☐ Known Personally

☐ Driver's License

☐ Other:

ID Number:

Issued By:

Date Issued:    Expiration Date:

Witness Full Name:    Phone Number:

Email Address:    Witness Signature:    Thumbprint:

Address:

Document Type:    Date/Time Notarized:    Document Date:

Comments:

# NOTARY LOG

| | | |
|---|---|---|
| Full Name | Phone Number: | Record Number: **115** |
| Email Address: | Signer's Signature: | $ Amount charged: |
| Address: | | Method of Payment: |
| | Gas & Mileage: | ☐ Cash  ☐ Credit  ☐ Check |
| Notary Service(s) Provided: | Identification: | ID Number: |
| ☐ Jurat | ☐ ID Card  ☐ Credible Witness | Issued By: |
| ☐ Oath/Affirmations | ☐ Passport  ☐ Known Personally | Date Issued:  Expiration Date: |
| ☐ Acknowledgment | ☐ Driver's License | |
| ☐ Other: | ☐ Other: | |

Witness Full Name:

Email Address: | Witness Signature: | Thumbprint:

Address:

Document Type: | Date/Time Notarized: | Document Date:

Comments:

# NOTARY LOG

| | | |
|---|---|---|
| Full Name | Phone Number: | Record Number: **116** |
| Email Address: | Signer's Signature: | $ Amount charged: |
| Address: | | Method of Payment: |
| | Gas & Mileage: | ☐ Cash  ☐ Credit  ☐ Check |
| Notary Service(s) Provided: | Identification: | ID Number: |
| ☐ Jurat | ☐ ID Card  ☐ Credible Witness | Issued By: |
| ☐ Oath/Affirmations | ☐ Passport  ☐ Known Personally | Date Issued:  Expiration Date: |
| ☐ Acknowledgment | ☐ Driver's License | |
| ☐ Other: | ☐ Other: | |

Witness Full Name:

Email Address: | Witness Signature: | Thumbprint:

Address:

Document Type: | Date/Time Notarized: | Document Date:

Comments:

## NOTARY LOG

| Full Name | Phone Number: | Record Number: **117** |
|---|---|---|
| Email Address: | Signer's Signature: | $ Amount charged: |
| Address: | | Method of Payment: |
| | Gas & Mileage: | ☐ Cash  ☐ Credit  ☐ Check |

| Notary Service(s) Provided: | Identification: | ID Number: |
|---|---|---|
| ☐ Jurat | ☐ ID Card  ☐ Credible Witness | Issued By: |
| ☐ Oath/Affirmations | ☐ Passport  ☐ Known Personally | Date Issued: / Expiration Date: |
| ☐ Acknowledgment | ☐ Driver's License | |
| ☐ Other: | ☐ Other: | |

| Witness Full Name: | Phone Number: | |
|---|---|---|
| Email Address: | Witness Signature: | Thumbprint: |
| Address: | | |

| Document Type: | Date/Time Notarized: | Document Date: |
|---|---|---|

Comments:

---

## NOTARY LOG

| Full Name | Phone Number: | Record Number: **118** |
|---|---|---|
| Email Address: | Signer's Signature: | $ Amount charged: |
| Address: | | Method of Payment: |
| | Gas & Mileage: | ☐ Cash  ☐ Credit  ☐ Check |

| Notary Service(s) Provided: | Identification: | ID Number: |
|---|---|---|
| ☐ Jurat | ☐ ID Card  ☐ Credible Witness | Issued By: |
| ☐ Oath/Affirmations | ☐ Passport  ☐ Known Personally | Date Issued: / Expiration Date: |
| ☐ Acknowledgment | ☐ Driver's License | |
| ☐ Other: | ☐ Other: | |

| Witness Full Name: | Phone Number: | |
|---|---|---|
| Email Address: | Witness Signature: | Thumbprint: |
| Address: | | |

| Document Type: | Date/Time Notarized: | Document Date: |
|---|---|---|

Comments:

## NOTARY LOG

| Full Name | Phone Number: | Record Number: **119** |
|---|---|---|
| Email Address: | Signer's Signature: | $ Amount charged: |
| Address: | | Method of Payment: |
| | Gas & Mileage: | ☐ Cash  ☐ Credit  ☐ Check |

| Notary Service(s) Provided: | Identification: | ID Number: |
|---|---|---|
| ☐ Jurat | ☐ ID Card  ☐ Credible Witness | Issued By: |
| ☐ Oath/Affirmations | ☐ Passport  ☐ Known Personally | Date Issued: / Expiration Date: |
| ☐ Acknowledgment | ☐ Driver's License | |
| ☐ Other: | ☐ Other: | |

| Witness Full Name: | Phone Number: | |
|---|---|---|
| Email Address: | Witness Signature: | Thumbprint: |
| Address: | | |

| Document Type: | Date/Time Notarized: | Document Date: |
|---|---|---|
| Comments: | | |

---

## NOTARY LOG

| Full Name | Phone Number: | Record Number: **120** |
|---|---|---|
| Email Address: | Signer's Signature: | $ Amount charged: |
| Address: | | Method of Payment: |
| | Gas & Mileage: | ☐ Cash  ☐ Credit  ☐ Check |

| Notary Service(s) Provided: | Identification: | ID Number: |
|---|---|---|
| ☐ Jurat | ☐ ID Card  ☐ Credible Witness | Issued By: |
| ☐ Oath/Affirmations | ☐ Passport  ☐ Known Personally | Date Issued: / Expiration Date: |
| ☐ Acknowledgment | ☐ Driver's License | |
| ☐ Other: | ☐ Other: | |

| Witness Full Name: | Phone Number: | |
|---|---|---|
| Email Address: | Witness Signature: | Thumbprint: |
| Address: | | |

| Document Type: | Date/Time Notarized: | Document Date: |
|---|---|---|
| Comments: | | |

## NOTARY LOG

| Full Name | Phone Number: | Record Number: **121** |
|---|---|---|
| Email Address: | Signer's Signature: | $ Amount charged: |
| Address: | | Method of Payment: |
| | Gas & Mileage: | ☐ Cash  ☐ Credit  ☐ Check |

| Notary Service(s) Provided: | Identification: | ID Number: |
|---|---|---|
| ☐ Jurat | ☐ ID Card   ☐ Credible Witness | Issued By: |
| ☐ Oath/Affirmations | ☐ Passport   ☐ Known Personally | Date Issued:   Expiration Date: |
| ☐ Acknowledgment | ☐ Driver's License | |
| ☐ Other: | ☐ Other: | |

| Witness Full Name: | Phone Number: | |
|---|---|---|
| Email Address: | Witness Signature: | Thumbprint: |
| Address: | | |

| Document Type: | Date/Time Notarized: | Document Date: |
|---|---|---|

Comments:

---

## NOTARY LOG

| Full Name | Phone Number: | Record Number: **122** |
|---|---|---|
| Email Address: | Signer's Signature: | $ Amount charged: |
| Address: | | Method of Payment: |
| | Gas & Mileage: | ☐ Cash  ☐ Credit  ☐ Check |

| Notary Service(s) Provided: | Identification: | ID Number: |
|---|---|---|
| ☐ Jurat | ☐ ID Card   ☐ Credible Witness | Issued By: |
| ☐ Oath/Affirmations | ☐ Passport   ☐ Known Personally | Date Issued:   Expiration Date: |
| ☐ Acknowledgment | ☐ Driver's License | |
| ☐ Other: | ☐ Other: | |

| Witness Full Name: | Phone Number: | |
|---|---|---|
| Email Address: | Witness Signature: | Thumbprint: |
| Address: | | |

| Document Type: | Date/Time Notarized: | Document Date: |
|---|---|---|

Comments:

## NOTARY LOG

| Full Name | Phone Number: | Record Number: **123** |
|---|---|---|
| Email Address: | Signer's Signature: | $ Amount charged: |
| Address: | | Method of Payment: |
| | Gas & Mileage: | ☐ Cash  ☐ Credit  ☐ Check |

Notary Service(s) Provided:

☐ Jurat

☐ Oath/Affirmations

☐ Acknowledgment

☐ Other:

Identification:

☐ ID Card  ☐ Credible Witness

☐ Passport  ☐ Known Personally

☐ Driver's License

☐ Other:

ID Number:

Issued By:

Date Issued:  Expiration Date:

Witness Full Name:

Phone Number:

Email Address:

Address:

Witness Signature:

Thumbprint:

Document Type:  Date/Time Notarized:  Document Date:

Comments:

---

## NOTARY LOG

| Full Name | Phone Number: | Record Number: **124** |
|---|---|---|
| Email Address: | Signer's Signature: | $ Amount charged: |
| Address: | | Method of Payment: |
| | Gas & Mileage: | ☐ Cash  ☐ Credit  ☐ Check |

Notary Service(s) Provided:

☐ Jurat

☐ Oath/Affirmations

☐ Acknowledgment

☐ Other:

Identification:

☐ ID Card  ☐ Credible Witness

☐ Passport  ☐ Known Personally

☐ Driver's License

☐ Other:

ID Number:

Issued By:

Date Issued:  Expiration Date:

Witness Full Name:

Phone Number:

Email Address:

Address:

Witness Signature:

Thumbprint:

Document Type:  Date/Time Notarized:  Document Date:

Comments:

## NOTARY LOG

| Full Name | Phone Number: | Record Number: **125** |
|---|---|---|
| Email Address: | Signer's Signature: | $ Amount charged: |
| Address: | | Method of Payment: |
| | Gas & Mileage: | ☐ Cash  ☐ Credit  ☐ Check |

| Notary Service(s) Provided: | Identification: | ID Number: |
|---|---|---|
| ☐ Jurat | ☐ ID Card  ☐ Credible Witness | Issued By: |
| ☐ Oath/Affirmations | ☐ Passport  ☐ Known Personally | Date Issued: / Expiration Date: |
| ☐ Acknowledgment | ☐ Driver's License | |
| ☐ Other: | ☐ Other: | |

| Witness Full Name: | Phone Number: | |
|---|---|---|
| Email Address: | Witness Signature: | Thumbprint: |
| Address: | | |

| Document Type: | Date/Time Notarized: | Document Date: |
|---|---|---|
| Comments: | | |

## NOTARY LOG

| Full Name | Phone Number: | Record Number: **126** |
|---|---|---|
| Email Address: | Signer's Signature: | $ Amount charged: |
| Address: | | Method of Payment: |
| | Gas & Mileage: | ☐ Cash  ☐ Credit  ☐ Check |

| Notary Service(s) Provided: | Identification: | ID Number: |
|---|---|---|
| ☐ Jurat | ☐ ID Card  ☐ Credible Witness | Issued By: |
| ☐ Oath/Affirmations | ☐ Passport  ☐ Known Personally | Date Issued: / Expiration Date: |
| ☐ Acknowledgment | ☐ Driver's License | |
| ☐ Other: | ☐ Other: | |

| Witness Full Name: | Phone Number: | |
|---|---|---|
| Email Address: | Witness Signature: | Thumbprint: |
| Address: | | |

| Document Type: | Date/Time Notarized: | Document Date: |
|---|---|---|
| Comments: | | |

## NOTARY LOG

| Full Name | Phone Number: | Record Number: **127** |
|---|---|---|
| Email Address: | Signer's Signature: | $ Amount charged: |
| Address: | | Method of Payment: |
| | Gas & Mileage: | ☐ Cash  ☐ Credit  ☐ Check |

| Notary Service(s) Provided: | Identification: | ID Number: |
|---|---|---|
| ☐ Jurat | ☐ ID Card  ☐ Credible Witness | Issued By: |
| ☐ Oath/Affirmations | ☐ Passport  ☐ Known Personally | Date Issued:  Expiration Date: |
| ☐ Acknowledgment | ☐ Driver's License | |
| ☐ Other: | ☐ Other: | |

| Witness Full Name: | Phone Number: | |
|---|---|---|
| Email Address: | Witness Signature: | Thumbprint: |
| Address: | | |

| Document Type: | Date/Time Notarized: | Document Date: |
|---|---|---|
| Comments: | | |

## NOTARY LOG

| Full Name | Phone Number: | Record Number: **128** |
|---|---|---|
| Email Address: | Signer's Signature: | $ Amount charged: |
| Address: | | Method of Payment: |
| | Gas & Mileage: | ☐ Cash  ☐ Credit  ☐ Check |

| Notary Service(s) Provided: | Identification: | ID Number: |
|---|---|---|
| ☐ Jurat | ☐ ID Card  ☐ Credible Witness | Issued By: |
| ☐ Oath/Affirmations | ☐ Passport  ☐ Known Personally | Date Issued:  Expiration Date: |
| ☐ Acknowledgment | ☐ Driver's License | |
| ☐ Other: | ☐ Other: | |

| Witness Full Name: | Phone Number: | |
|---|---|---|
| Email Address: | Witness Signature: | Thumbprint: |
| Address: | | |

| Document Type: | Date/Time Notarized: | Document Date: |
|---|---|---|
| Comments: | | |

## NOTARY LOG

| Full Name | Phone Number: | Record Number: **129** |
|---|---|---|
| Email Address: | Signer's Signature: | $ Amount charged: |
| Address: | | Method of Payment: |
| | Gas & Mileage: | ☐ Cash   ☐ Credit   ☐ Check |

| Notary Service(s) Provided: | Identification: | ID Number: |
|---|---|---|
| ☐ Jurat | ☐ ID Card   ☐ Credible Witness | Issued By: |
| ☐ Oath/Affirmations | ☐ Passport   ☐ Known Personally | Date Issued:   Expiration Date: |
| ☐ Acknowledgment | ☐ Driver's License | |
| ☐ Other: | ☐ Other: | |

| Witness Full Name: | Phone Number: | |
|---|---|---|
| Email Address: | Witness Signature: | Thumbprint: |
| Address: | | |

| Document Type: | Date/Time Notarized: | Document Date: |
|---|---|---|
| Comments: | | |

## NOTARY LOG

| Full Name | Phone Number: | Record Number: **130** |
|---|---|---|
| Email Address: | Signer's Signature: | $ Amount charged: |
| Address: | | Method of Payment: |
| | Gas & Mileage: | ☐ Cash   ☐ Credit   ☐ Check |

| Notary Service(s) Provided: | Identification: | ID Number: |
|---|---|---|
| ☐ Jurat | ☐ ID Card   ☐ Credible Witness | Issued By: |
| ☐ Oath/Affirmations | ☐ Passport   ☐ Known Personally | Date Issued:   Expiration Date: |
| ☐ Acknowledgment | ☐ Driver's License | |
| ☐ Other: | ☐ Other: | |

| Witness Full Name: | Phone Number: | |
|---|---|---|
| Email Address: | Witness Signature: | Thumbprint: |
| Address: | | |

| Document Type: | Date/Time Notarized: | Document Date: |
|---|---|---|
| Comments: | | |

## NOTARY LOG

| | | |
|---|---|---|
| Full Name | Phone Number: | Record Number: **131** |
| Email Address: | Signer's Signature: | $ Amount charged: |
| Address: | | Method of Payment: |
| | Gas & Mileage: | ☐ Cash  ☐ Credit  ☐ Check |
| Notary Service(s) Provided: | Identification: | ID Number: |
| ☐ Jurat | ☐ ID Card   ☐ Credible Witness | Issued By: |
| ☐ Oath/Affirmations | ☐ Passport   ☐ Known Personally | Date Issued:   Expiration Date: |
| ☐ Acknowledgment | ☐ Driver's License | |
| ☐ Other: | ☐ Other: | |

| | | |
|---|---|---|
| Witness Full Name: | Phone Number: | |
| Email Address: | Witness Signature: | Thumbprint: |
| Address: | | |
| Document Type: | Date/Time Notarized: | Document Date: |
| Comments: | | |

## NOTARY LOG

| | | |
|---|---|---|
| Full Name | Phone Number: | Record Number: **132** |
| Email Address: | Signer's Signature: | $ Amount charged: |
| Address: | | Method of Payment: |
| | Gas & Mileage: | ☐ Cash  ☐ Credit  ☐ Check |
| Notary Service(s) Provided: | Identification: | ID Number: |
| ☐ Jurat | ☐ ID Card   ☐ Credible Witness | Issued By: |
| ☐ Oath/Affirmations | ☐ Passport   ☐ Known Personally | Date Issued:   Expiration Date: |
| ☐ Acknowledgment | ☐ Driver's License | |
| ☐ Other: | ☐ Other: | |

| | | |
|---|---|---|
| Witness Full Name: | Phone Number: | |
| Email Address: | Witness Signature: | Thumbprint: |
| Address: | | |
| Document Type: | Date/Time Notarized: | Document Date: |
| Comments: | | |

## NOTARY LOG

| Full Name | Phone Number: | Record Number: **133** |
|---|---|---|
| Email Address: | Signer's Signature: | $ Amount charged: |
| Address: | | Method of Payment: |
| | Gas & Mileage: | ☐ Cash  ☐ Credit  ☐ Check |

| Notary Service(s) Provided: | Identification: | ID Number: |
|---|---|---|
| ☐ Jurat | ☐ ID Card  ☐ Credible Witness | Issued By: |
| ☐ Oath/Affirmations | ☐ Passport  ☐ Known Personally | Date Issued: | Expiration Date: |
| ☐ Acknowledgment | ☐ Driver's License | | |
| ☐ Other: | ☐ Other: | | |

| Witness Full Name: | Phone Number: | |
|---|---|---|
| Email Address: | Witness Signature: | Thumbprint: |
| Address: | | |

| Document Type: | Date/Time Notarized: | Document Date: |
|---|---|---|

Comments:

---

## NOTARY LOG

| Full Name | Phone Number: | Record Number: **134** |
|---|---|---|
| Email Address: | Signer's Signature: | $ Amount charged: |
| Address: | | Method of Payment: |
| | Gas & Mileage: | ☐ Cash  ☐ Credit  ☐ Check |

| Notary Service(s) Provided: | Identification: | ID Number: |
|---|---|---|
| ☐ Jurat | ☐ ID Card  ☐ Credible Witness | Issued By: |
| ☐ Oath/Affirmations | ☐ Passport  ☐ Known Personally | Date Issued: | Expiration Date: |
| ☐ Acknowledgment | ☐ Driver's License | | |
| ☐ Other: | ☐ Other: | | |

| Witness Full Name: | Phone Number: | |
|---|---|---|
| Email Address: | Witness Signature: | Thumbprint: |
| Address: | | |

| Document Type: | Date/Time Notarized: | Document Date: |
|---|---|---|

Comments:

## NOTARY LOG

| Full Name | Phone Number: | Record Number: **135** |
|---|---|---|
| Email Address: | Signer's Signature: | $ Amount charged: |
| Address: | | Method of Payment: |
| | Gas & Mileage: | ☐ Cash  ☐ Credit  ☐ Check |

| Notary Service(s) Provided: | Identification: | ID Number: |
|---|---|---|
| ☐ Jurat | ☐ ID Card   ☐ Credible Witness | Issued By: |
| ☐ Oath/Affirmations | ☐ Passport   ☐ Known Personally | Date Issued:   Expiration Date: |
| ☐ Acknowledgment | ☐ Driver's License | |
| ☐ Other: | ☐ Other: | |

| Witness Full Name: | Phone Number: | |
|---|---|---|
| Email Address: | Witness Signature: | Thumbprint: |
| Address: | | |

| Document Type: | Date/Time Notarized: | Document Date: |
|---|---|---|
| Comments: | | |

## NOTARY LOG

| Full Name | Phone Number: | Record Number: **136** |
|---|---|---|
| Email Address: | Signer's Signature: | $ Amount charged: |
| Address: | | Method of Payment: |
| | Gas & Mileage: | ☐ Cash  ☐ Credit  ☐ Check |

| Notary Service(s) Provided: | Identification: | ID Number: |
|---|---|---|
| ☐ Jurat | ☐ ID Card   ☐ Credible Witness | Issued By: |
| ☐ Oath/Affirmations | ☐ Passport   ☐ Known Personally | Date Issued:   Expiration Date: |
| ☐ Acknowledgment | ☐ Driver's License | |
| ☐ Other: | ☐ Other: | |

| Witness Full Name: | Phone Number: | |
|---|---|---|
| Email Address: | Witness Signature: | Thumbprint: |
| Address: | | |

| Document Type: | Date/Time Notarized: | Document Date: |
|---|---|---|
| Comments: | | |

## NOTARY LOG

| Full Name | Phone Number: | Record Number: **137** |
|---|---|---|
| Email Address: | Signer's Signature: | $ Amount charged: |
| Address: | | Method of Payment: |
| | Gas & Mileage: | ☐ Cash  ☐ Credit  ☐ Check |

| Notary Service(s) Provided: | Identification: | ID Number: |
|---|---|---|
| ☐ Jurat | ☐ ID Card   ☐ Credible Witness | Issued By: |
| ☐ Oath/Affirmations | ☐ Passport   ☐ Known Personally | Date Issued: | Expiration Date: |
| ☐ Acknowledgment | ☐ Driver's License | | |
| ☐ Other: | ☐ Other: | | |

| Witness Full Name: | Phone Number: | |
|---|---|---|
| Email Address: | Witness Signature: | Thumbprint: |
| Address: | | |

| Document Type: | Date/Time Notarized: | Document Date: | |
|---|---|---|---|
| Comments: | | | |

---

## NOTARY LOG

| Full Name | Phone Number: | Record Number: **138** |
|---|---|---|
| Email Address: | Signer's Signature: | $ Amount charged: |
| Address: | | Method of Payment: |
| | Gas & Mileage: | ☐ Cash  ☐ Credit  ☐ Check |

| Notary Service(s) Provided: | Identification: | ID Number: |
|---|---|---|
| ☐ Jurat | ☐ ID Card   ☐ Credible Witness | Issued By: |
| ☐ Oath/Affirmations | ☐ Passport   ☐ Known Personally | Date Issued: | Expiration Date: |
| ☐ Acknowledgment | ☐ Driver's License | | |
| ☐ Other: | ☐ Other: | | |

| Witness Full Name: | Phone Number: | |
|---|---|---|
| Email Address: | Witness Signature: | Thumbprint: |
| Address: | | |

| Document Type: | Date/Time Notarized: | Document Date: | |
|---|---|---|---|
| Comments: | | | |

## NOTARY LOG

| | | |
|---|---|---|
| Full Name | Phone Number: | Record Number: **139** |
| Email Address: | Signer's Signature: | $ Amount charged: |
| Address: | | Method of Payment: |
| | Gas & Mileage: | ☐ Cash   ☐ Credit   ☐ Check |
| Notary Service(s) Provided: | Identification: | ID Number: |
| ☐ Jurat | ☐ ID Card     ☐ Credible Witness | Issued By: |
| ☐ Oath/Affirmations | ☐ Passport    ☐ Known Personally | Date Issued:   Expiration Date: |
| ☐ Acknowledgment | ☐ Driver's License | |
| ☐ Other: | ☐ Other: | |

| | | |
|---|---|---|
| Witness Full Name: | Phone Number: | |
| Email Address: | Witness Signature: | Thumbprint: |
| Address: | | |
| Document Type: | Date/Time Notarized: | Document Date: |
| Comments: | | |

## NOTARY LOG

| | | |
|---|---|---|
| Full Name | Phone Number: | Record Number: **140** |
| Email Address: | Signer's Signature: | $ Amount charged: |
| Address: | | Method of Payment: |
| | Gas & Mileage: | ☐ Cash   ☐ Credit   ☐ Check |
| Notary Service(s) Provided: | Identification: | ID Number: |
| ☐ Jurat | ☐ ID Card     ☐ Credible Witness | Issued By: |
| ☐ Oath/Affirmations | ☐ Passport    ☐ Known Personally | Date Issued:   Expiration Date: |
| ☐ Acknowledgment | ☐ Driver's License | |
| ☐ Other: | ☐ Other: | |

| | | |
|---|---|---|
| Witness Full Name: | Phone Number: | |
| Email Address: | Witness Signature: | Thumbprint: |
| Address: | | |
| Document Type: | Date/Time Notarized: | Document Date: |
| Comments: | | |

## NOTARY LOG

| Full Name | Phone Number: | Record Number: **141** |
|---|---|---|
| Email Address: | Signer's Signature: | $ Amount charged: |
| Address: | | Method of Payment: |
| | Gas & Mileage: | ☐ Cash    ☐ Credit    ☐ Check |

| Notary Service(s) Provided: | Identification: | ID Number: |
|---|---|---|
| ☐ Jurat | ☐ ID Card    ☐ Credible Witness | Issued By: |
| ☐ Oath/Affirmations | ☐ Passport    ☐ Known Personally | Date Issued:    Expiration Date: |
| ☐ Acknowledgment | ☐ Driver's License | |
| ☐ Other: | ☐ Other: | |

| Witness Full Name: | Phone Number: | |
|---|---|---|
| Email Address: | Witness Signature: | Thumbprint: |
| Address: | | |

| Document Type: | Date/Time Notarized: | Document Date: |
|---|---|---|

Comments:

---

## NOTARY LOG

| Full Name | Phone Number: | Record Number: **142** |
|---|---|---|
| Email Address: | Signer's Signature: | $ Amount charged: |
| Address: | | Method of Payment: |
| | Gas & Mileage: | ☐ Cash    ☐ Credit    ☐ Check |

| Notary Service(s) Provided: | Identification: | ID Number: |
|---|---|---|
| ☐ Jurat | ☐ ID Card    ☐ Credible Witness | Issued By: |
| ☐ Oath/Affirmations | ☐ Passport    ☐ Known Personally | Date Issued:    Expiration Date: |
| ☐ Acknowledgment | ☐ Driver's License | |
| ☐ Other: | ☐ Other: | |

| Witness Full Name: | Phone Number: | |
|---|---|---|
| Email Address: | Witness Signature: | Thumbprint: |
| Address: | | |

| Document Type: | Date/Time Notarized: | Document Date: |
|---|---|---|

Comments:

## NOTARY LOG

| | | |
|---|---|---|
| Full Name | Phone Number: | Record Number: **143** |
| Email Address: | Signer's Signature: | $ Amount charged: |
| Address: | | Method of Payment: |
| | Gas & Mileage: | ☐ Cash  ☐ Credit  ☐ Check |
| Notary Service(s) Provided: | Identification: | ID Number: |
| ☐ Jurat | ☐ ID Card   ☐ Credible Witness | Issued By: |
| ☐ Oath/Affirmations | ☐ Passport   ☐ Known Personally | Date Issued:   Expiration Date: |
| ☐ Acknowledgment | ☐ Driver's License | |
| ☐ Other: | ☐ Other: | |
| Witness Full Name: | Phone Number: | |
| Email Address: | Witness Signature: | Thumbprint: |
| Address: | | |
| Document Type: | Date/Time Notarized: | Document Date: |
| Comments: | | |

## NOTARY LOG

| | | |
|---|---|---|
| Full Name | Phone Number: | Record Number: **144** |
| Email Address: | Signer's Signature: | $ Amount charged: |
| Address: | | Method of Payment: |
| | Gas & Mileage: | ☐ Cash  ☐ Credit  ☐ Check |
| Notary Service(s) Provided: | Identification: | ID Number: |
| ☐ Jurat | ☐ ID Card   ☐ Credible Witness | Issued By: |
| ☐ Oath/Affirmations | ☐ Passport   ☐ Known Personally | Date Issued:   Expiration Date: |
| ☐ Acknowledgment | ☐ Driver's License | |
| ☐ Other: | ☐ Other: | |
| Witness Full Name: | Phone Number: | |
| Email Address: | Witness Signature: | Thumbprint: |
| Address: | | |
| Document Type: | Date/Time Notarized: | Document Date: |
| Comments: | | |

## NOTARY LOG

| Full Name | Phone Number: | Record Number: **145** |
|---|---|---|
| Email Address: | Signer's Signature: | $ Amount charged: |
| Address: | | Method of Payment: |
| | Gas & Mileage: | ☐ Cash   ☐ Credit   ☐ Check |

| Notary Service(s) Provided: | Identification: | | ID Number: | |
|---|---|---|---|---|
| ☐ Jurat | ☐ ID Card | ☐ Credible Witness | Issued By: | |
| ☐ Oath/Affirmations | ☐ Passport | ☐ Known Personally | Date Issued: | Expiration Date: |
| ☐ Acknowledgment | ☐ Driver's License | | | |
| ☐ Other: | ☐ Other: | | | |

| Witness Full Name: | Phone Number: | |
|---|---|---|
| Email Address: | Witness Signature: | Thumbprint: |
| Address: | | |

| Document Type: | Date/Time Notarized: | Document Date: | |
|---|---|---|---|
| Comments: | | | |

## NOTARY LOG

| Full Name | Phone Number: | Record Number: **146** |
|---|---|---|
| Email Address: | Signer's Signature: | $ Amount charged: |
| Address: | | Method of Payment: |
| | Gas & Mileage: | ☐ Cash   ☐ Credit   ☐ Check |

| Notary Service(s) Provided: | Identification: | | ID Number: | |
|---|---|---|---|---|
| ☐ Jurat | ☐ ID Card | ☐ Credible Witness | Issued By: | |
| ☐ Oath/Affirmations | ☐ Passport | ☐ Known Personally | Date Issued: | Expiration Date: |
| ☐ Acknowledgment | ☐ Driver's License | | | |
| ☐ Other: | ☐ Other: | | | |

| Witness Full Name: | Phone Number: | |
|---|---|---|
| Email Address: | Witness Signature: | Thumbprint: |
| Address: | | |

| Document Type: | Date/Time Notarized: | Document Date: | |
|---|---|---|---|
| Comments: | | | |

## NOTARY LOG

| Full Name | Phone Number: | Record Number: **147** |
|---|---|---|
| Email Address: | Signer's Signature: | $ Amount charged: |
| Address: | | Method of Payment: |
| | Gas & Mileage: | ☐ Cash    ☐ Credit    ☐ Check |

| Notary Service(s) Provided: | Identification: | ID Number: |
|---|---|---|
| ☐ Jurat | ☐ ID Card    ☐ Credible Witness | Issued By: |
| ☐ Oath/Affirmations | ☐ Passport    ☐ Known Personally | Date Issued: / Expiration Date: |
| ☐ Acknowledgment | ☐ Driver's License | |
| ☐ Other: | ☐ Other: | |

Witness Full Name:       Phone Number:

| Email Address: | Witness Signature: | Thumbprint: |
|---|---|---|
| Address: | | |

Document Type:    Date/Time Notarized:    Document Date:

Comments:

---

## NOTARY LOG

| Full Name | Phone Number: | Record Number: **148** |
|---|---|---|
| Email Address: | Signer's Signature: | $ Amount charged: |
| Address: | | Method of Payment: |
| | Gas & Mileage: | ☐ Cash    ☐ Credit    ☐ Check |

| Notary Service(s) Provided: | Identification: | ID Number: |
|---|---|---|
| ☐ Jurat | ☐ ID Card    ☐ Credible Witness | Issued By: |
| ☐ Oath/Affirmations | ☐ Passport    ☐ Known Personally | Date Issued: / Expiration Date: |
| ☐ Acknowledgment | ☐ Driver's License | |
| ☐ Other: | ☐ Other: | |

Witness Full Name:       Phone Number:

| Email Address: | Witness Signature: | Thumbprint: |
|---|---|---|
| Address: | | |

Document Type:    Date/Time Notarized:    Document Date:

Comments:

## NOTARY LOG

| Full Name | Phone Number: | Record Number: **149** |
|---|---|---|
| Email Address: | Signer's Signature: | $ Amount charged: |
| Address: | | Method of Payment: |
| | Gas & Mileage: | ☐ Cash  ☐ Credit  ☐ Check |

| Notary Service(s) Provided: | Identification: | ID Number: |
|---|---|---|
| ☐ Jurat | ☐ ID Card   ☐ Credible Witness | Issued By: |
| ☐ Oath/Affirmations | ☐ Passport   ☐ Known Personally | Date Issued:   Expiration Date: |
| ☐ Acknowledgment | ☐ Driver's License | |
| ☐ Other: | ☐ Other: | |

| Witness Full Name: | Phone Number: | |
|---|---|---|
| Email Address: | Witness Signature: | Thumbprint: |
| Address: | | |

| Document Type: | Date/Time Notarized: | Document Date: |
|---|---|---|
| Comments: | | |

---

## NOTARY LOG

| Full Name | Phone Number: | Record Number: **150** |
|---|---|---|
| Email Address: | Signer's Signature: | $ Amount charged: |
| Address: | | Method of Payment: |
| | Gas & Mileage: | ☐ Cash  ☐ Credit  ☐ Check |

| Notary Service(s) Provided: | Identification: | ID Number: |
|---|---|---|
| ☐ Jurat | ☐ ID Card   ☐ Credible Witness | Issued By: |
| ☐ Oath/Affirmations | ☐ Passport   ☐ Known Personally | Date Issued:   Expiration Date: |
| ☐ Acknowledgment | ☐ Driver's License | |
| ☐ Other: | ☐ Other: | |

| Witness Full Name: | Phone Number: | |
|---|---|---|
| Email Address: | Witness Signature: | Thumbprint: |
| Address: | | |

| Document Type: | Date/Time Notarized: | Document Date: |
|---|---|---|
| Comments: | | |

## NOTARY LOG

| Full Name | Phone Number: | Record Number: **151** |
|---|---|---|
| Email Address: | Signer's Signature: | $ Amount charged: |
| Address: | | Method of Payment: |
| | Gas & Mileage: | ☐ Cash  ☐ Credit  ☐ Check |
| Notary Service(s) Provided: | Identification: | ID Number: |
| ☐ Jurat | ☐ ID Card  ☐ Credible Witness | Issued By: |
| ☐ Oath/Affirmations | ☐ Passport  ☐ Known Personally | Date Issued: | Expiration Date: |
| ☐ Acknowledgment | ☐ Driver's License | | |
| ☐ Other: | ☐ Other: | | |

| Witness Full Name: | Phone Number: | |
|---|---|---|
| Email Address: | Witness Signature: | Thumbprint: |
| Address: | | |
| Document Type: | Date/Time Notarized: | Document Date: | |
| Comments: | | | |

## NOTARY LOG

| Full Name | Phone Number: | Record Number: **152** |
|---|---|---|
| Email Address: | Signer's Signature: | $ Amount charged: |
| Address: | | Method of Payment: |
| | Gas & Mileage: | ☐ Cash  ☐ Credit  ☐ Check |
| Notary Service(s) Provided: | Identification: | ID Number: |
| ☐ Jurat | ☐ ID Card  ☐ Credible Witness | Issued By: |
| ☐ Oath/Affirmations | ☐ Passport  ☐ Known Personally | Date Issued: | Expiration Date: |
| ☐ Acknowledgment | ☐ Driver's License | | |
| ☐ Other: | ☐ Other: | | |

| Witness Full Name: | Phone Number: | |
|---|---|---|
| Email Address: | Witness Signature: | Thumbprint: |
| Address: | | |
| Document Type: | Date/Time Notarized: | Document Date: | |
| Comments: | | | |

## NOTARY LOG

| Full Name | Phone Number: | Record Number: **153** |
|---|---|---|
| Email Address: | Signer's Signature: | $ Amount charged: |
| Address: | | Method of Payment: |
| | Gas & Mileage: | ☐ Cash   ☐ Credit   ☐ Check |
| Notary Service(s) Provided: | Identification: | ID Number: |
| ☐ Jurat | ☐ ID Card   ☐ Credible Witness | Issued By: |
| ☐ Oath/Affirmations | ☐ Passport   ☐ Known Personally | Date Issued: | Expiration Date: |
| ☐ Acknowledgment | ☐ Driver's License | | |
| ☐ Other: | ☐ Other: | | |

| Witness Full Name: | Phone Number: | |
|---|---|---|
| Email Address: | Witness Signature: | Thumbprint: |
| Address: | | |
| Document Type: | Date/Time Notarized: | Document Date: | |
| Comments: | | | |

## NOTARY LOG

| Full Name | Phone Number: | Record Number: **154** |
|---|---|---|
| Email Address: | Signer's Signature: | $ Amount charged: |
| Address: | | Method of Payment: |
| | Gas & Mileage: | ☐ Cash   ☐ Credit   ☐ Check |
| Notary Service(s) Provided: | Identification: | ID Number: |
| ☐ Jurat | ☐ ID Card   ☐ Credible Witness | Issued By: |
| ☐ Oath/Affirmations | ☐ Passport   ☐ Known Personally | Date Issued: | Expiration Date: |
| ☐ Acknowledgment | ☐ Driver's License | | |
| ☐ Other: | ☐ Other: | | |

| Witness Full Name: | Phone Number: | |
|---|---|---|
| Email Address: | Witness Signature: | Thumbprint: |
| Address: | | |
| Document Type: | Date/Time Notarized: | Document Date: | |
| Comments: | | | |

## NOTARY LOG

| Full Name | Phone Number: | Record Number: **155** |
|---|---|---|
| Email Address: | Signer's Signature: | $ Amount charged: |
| Address: | | Method of Payment: |
| | Gas & Mileage: | ☐ Cash    ☐ Credit    ☐ Check |

| Notary Service(s) Provided: | Identification: | ID Number: |
|---|---|---|
| ☐ Jurat | ☐ ID Card     ☐ Credible Witness | Issued By: |
| ☐ Oath/Affirmations | ☐ Passport    ☐ Known Personally | Date Issued:  |  Expiration Date: |
| ☐ Acknowledgment | ☐ Driver's License | |
| ☐ Other: | ☐ Other: | |

| Witness Full Name: | Phone Number: | |
|---|---|---|
| Email Address: | Witness Signature: | Thumbprint: |
| Address: | | |

| Document Type: | Date/Time Notarized: | Document Date: |
|---|---|---|
| Comments: | | |

## NOTARY LOG

| Full Name | Phone Number: | Record Number: **156** |
|---|---|---|
| Email Address: | Signer's Signature: | $ Amount charged: |
| Address: | | Method of Payment: |
| | Gas & Mileage: | ☐ Cash    ☐ Credit    ☐ Check |

| Notary Service(s) Provided: | Identification: | ID Number: |
|---|---|---|
| ☐ Jurat | ☐ ID Card     ☐ Credible Witness | Issued By: |
| ☐ Oath/Affirmations | ☐ Passport    ☐ Known Personally | Date Issued:  |  Expiration Date: |
| ☐ Acknowledgment | ☐ Driver's License | |
| ☐ Other: | ☐ Other: | |

| Witness Full Name: | Phone Number: | |
|---|---|---|
| Email Address: | Witness Signature: | Thumbprint: |
| Address: | | |

| Document Type: | Date/Time Notarized: | Document Date: |
|---|---|---|
| Comments: | | |

## NOTARY LOG

| Full Name | Phone Number: | Record Number: **157** |
|---|---|---|
| Email Address: | Signer's Signature: | $ Amount charged: |
| Address: | | Method of Payment: |
| | Gas & Mileage: | ☐ Cash ☐ Credit ☐ Check |

| Notary Service(s) Provided: | Identification: | ID Number: |
|---|---|---|
| ☐ Jurat | ☐ ID Card ☐ Credible Witness | Issued By: |
| ☐ Oath/Affirmations | ☐ Passport ☐ Known Personally | Date Issued: / Expiration Date: |
| ☐ Acknowledgment | ☐ Driver's License | |
| ☐ Other: | ☐ Other: | |

| Witness Full Name: | Phone Number: | |
|---|---|---|
| Email Address: | Witness Signature: | Thumbprint: |
| Address: | | |

| Document Type: | Date/Time Notarized: | Document Date: |
|---|---|---|

Comments:

---

## NOTARY LOG

| Full Name | Phone Number: | Record Number: **158** |
|---|---|---|
| Email Address: | Signer's Signature: | $ Amount charged: |
| Address: | | Method of Payment: |
| | Gas & Mileage: | ☐ Cash ☐ Credit ☐ Check |

| Notary Service(s) Provided: | Identification: | ID Number: |
|---|---|---|
| ☐ Jurat | ☐ ID Card ☐ Credible Witness | Issued By: |
| ☐ Oath/Affirmations | ☐ Passport ☐ Known Personally | Date Issued: / Expiration Date: |
| ☐ Acknowledgment | ☐ Driver's License | |
| ☐ Other: | ☐ Other: | |

| Witness Full Name: | Phone Number: | |
|---|---|---|
| Email Address: | Witness Signature: | Thumbprint: |
| Address: | | |

| Document Type: | Date/Time Notarized: | Document Date: |
|---|---|---|

Comments:

## NOTARY LOG

| | | |
|---|---|---|
| Full Name | Phone Number: | Record Number: **159** |
| Email Address: | Signer's Signature: | $ Amount charged: |
| Address: | | Method of Payment: |
| | Gas & Mileage: | ☐ Cash  ☐ Credit  ☐ Check |
| Notary Service(s) Provided: | Identification: | ID Number: |
| ☐ Jurat | ☐ ID Card   ☐ Credible Witness | Issued By: |
| ☐ Oath/Affirmations | ☐ Passport   ☐ Known Personally | Date Issued:   Expiration Date: |
| ☐ Acknowledgment | ☐ Driver's License | |
| ☐ Other: | ☐ Other: | |

| | | |
|---|---|---|
| Witness Full Name: | Phone Number: | |
| Email Address: | Witness Signature: | Thumbprint: |
| Address: | | |
| Document Type: | Date/Time Notarized: | Document Date: |
| Comments: | | |

## NOTARY LOG

| | | |
|---|---|---|
| Full Name | Phone Number: | Record Number: **160** |
| Email Address: | Signer's Signature: | $ Amount charged: |
| Address: | | Method of Payment: |
| | Gas & Mileage: | ☐ Cash  ☐ Credit  ☐ Check |
| Notary Service(s) Provided: | Identification: | ID Number: |
| ☐ Jurat | ☐ ID Card   ☐ Credible Witness | Issued By: |
| ☐ Oath/Affirmations | ☐ Passport   ☐ Known Personally | Date Issued:   Expiration Date: |
| ☐ Acknowledgment | ☐ Driver's License | |
| ☐ Other: | ☐ Other: | |

| | | |
|---|---|---|
| Witness Full Name: | Phone Number: | |
| Email Address: | Witness Signature: | Thumbprint: |
| Address: | | |
| Document Type: | Date/Time Notarized: | Document Date: |
| Comments: | | |

## NOTARY LOG

| Full Name | Phone Number: | Record Number: **161** |
|---|---|---|
| Email Address: | Signer's Signature: | $ Amount charged: |
| Address: | | Method of Payment: |
| | Gas & Mileage: | ☐ Cash  ☐ Credit  ☐ Check |

| Notary Service(s) Provided: | Identification: | ID Number: |
|---|---|---|
| ☐ Jurat | ☐ ID Card  ☐ Credible Witness | Issued By: |
| ☐ Oath/Affirmations | ☐ Passport  ☐ Known Personally | Date Issued:  Expiration Date: |
| ☐ Acknowledgment | ☐ Driver's License | |
| ☐ Other: | ☐ Other: | |

| Witness Full Name: | Phone Number: | |
|---|---|---|
| Email Address: | Witness Signature: | Thumbprint: |
| Address: | | |

| Document Type: | Date/Time Notarized: | Document Date: |
|---|---|---|

Comments:

---

## NOTARY LOG

| Full Name | Phone Number: | Record Number: **162** |
|---|---|---|
| Email Address: | Signer's Signature: | $ Amount charged: |
| Address: | | Method of Payment: |
| | Gas & Mileage: | ☐ Cash  ☐ Credit  ☐ Check |

| Notary Service(s) Provided: | Identification: | ID Number: |
|---|---|---|
| ☐ Jurat | ☐ ID Card  ☐ Credible Witness | Issued By: |
| ☐ Oath/Affirmations | ☐ Passport  ☐ Known Personally | Date Issued:  Expiration Date: |
| ☐ Acknowledgment | ☐ Driver's License | |
| ☐ Other: | ☐ Other: | |

| Witness Full Name: | Phone Number: | |
|---|---|---|
| Email Address: | Witness Signature: | Thumbprint: |
| Address: | | |

| Document Type: | Date/Time Notarized: | Document Date: |
|---|---|---|

Comments:

## NOTARY LOG

| | | |
|---|---|---|
| Full Name | Phone Number: | Record Number: **163** |
| Email Address: | Signer's Signature: | $ Amount charged: |
| Address: | | Method of Payment: |
| | Gas & Mileage: | ☐ Cash    ☐ Credit    ☐ Check |
| Notary Service(s) Provided: | Identification: | ID Number: |
| ☐ Jurat | ☐ ID Card    ☐ Credible Witness | Issued By: |
| ☐ Oath/Affirmations | ☐ Passport    ☐ Known Personally | Date Issued: | Expiration Date: |
| ☐ Acknowledgment | ☐ Driver's License | | |
| ☐ Other: | ☐ Other: | | |

| | | |
|---|---|---|
| Witness Full Name: | Phone Number: | |
| Email Address: | Witness Signature: | Thumbprint: |
| Address: | | |
| Document Type: | Date/Time Notarized: | Document Date: |
| Comments: | | |

## NOTARY LOG

| | | |
|---|---|---|
| Full Name | Phone Number: | Record Number: **164** |
| Email Address: | Signer's Signature: | $ Amount charged: |
| Address: | | Method of Payment: |
| | Gas & Mileage: | ☐ Cash    ☐ Credit    ☐ Check |
| Notary Service(s) Provided: | Identification: | ID Number: |
| ☐ Jurat | ☐ ID Card    ☐ Credible Witness | Issued By: |
| ☐ Oath/Affirmations | ☐ Passport    ☐ Known Personally | Date Issued: | Expiration Date: |
| ☐ Acknowledgment | ☐ Driver's License | | |
| ☐ Other: | ☐ Other: | | |

| | | |
|---|---|---|
| Witness Full Name: | Phone Number: | |
| Email Address: | Witness Signature: | Thumbprint: |
| Address: | | |
| Document Type: | Date/Time Notarized: | Document Date: |
| Comments: | | |

## NOTARY LOG

| Full Name | Phone Number: | Record Number: **165** |
|---|---|---|
| Email Address: | Signer's Signature: | $ Amount charged: |
| Address: | | Method of Payment: |
| | Gas & Mileage: | ☐ Cash  ☐ Credit  ☐ Check |
| Notary Service(s) Provided: | Identification: | ID Number: |
| ☐ Jurat | ☐ ID Card    ☐ Credible Witness | Issued By: |
| ☐ Oath/Affirmations | ☐ Passport    ☐ Known Personally | Date Issued:    Expiration Date: |
| ☐ Acknowledgment | ☐ Driver's License | |
| ☐ Other: | ☐ Other: | |

| Witness Full Name: | Phone Number: | |
|---|---|---|
| Email Address: | Witness Signature: | Thumbprint: |
| Address: | | |

| Document Type: | Date/Time Notarized: | Document Date: |
|---|---|---|
| Comments: | | |

## NOTARY LOG

| Full Name | Phone Number: | Record Number: **166** |
|---|---|---|
| Email Address: | Signer's Signature: | $ Amount charged: |
| Address: | | Method of Payment: |
| | Gas & Mileage: | ☐ Cash  ☐ Credit  ☐ Check |
| Notary Service(s) Provided: | Identification: | ID Number: |
| ☐ Jurat | ☐ ID Card    ☐ Credible Witness | Issued By: |
| ☐ Oath/Affirmations | ☐ Passport    ☐ Known Personally | Date Issued:    Expiration Date: |
| ☐ Acknowledgment | ☐ Driver's License | |
| ☐ Other: | ☐ Other: | |

| Witness Full Name: | Phone Number: | |
|---|---|---|
| Email Address: | Witness Signature: | Thumbprint: |
| Address: | | |

| Document Type: | Date/Time Notarized: | Document Date: |
|---|---|---|
| Comments: | | |

## NOTARY LOG

| | | |
|---|---|---|
| Full Name | Phone Number: | Record Number: **167** |
| Email Address: | Signer's Signature: | $ Amount charged: |
| Address: | | Method of Payment: |
| | Gas & Mileage: | ☐ Cash   ☐ Credit   ☐ Check |
| Notary Service(s) Provided: | Identification: | ID Number: |
| ☐ Jurat | ☐ ID Card   ☐ Credible Witness | Issued By: |
| ☐ Oath/Affirmations | ☐ Passport   ☐ Known Personally | Date Issued:   Expiration Date: |
| ☐ Acknowledgment | ☐ Driver's License | |
| ☐ Other: | ☐ Other: | |

| | | |
|---|---|---|
| Witness Full Name: | Phone Number: | |
| Email Address: | Witness Signature: | Thumbprint: |
| Address: | | |
| Document Type: | Date/Time Notarized: | Document Date: |
| Comments: | | |

## NOTARY LOG

| | | |
|---|---|---|
| Full Name | Phone Number: | Record Number: **168** |
| Email Address: | Signer's Signature: | $ Amount charged: |
| Address: | | Method of Payment: |
| | Gas & Mileage: | ☐ Cash   ☐ Credit   ☐ Check |
| Notary Service(s) Provided: | Identification: | ID Number: |
| ☐ Jurat | ☐ ID Card   ☐ Credible Witness | Issued By: |
| ☐ Oath/Affirmations | ☐ Passport   ☐ Known Personally | Date Issued:   Expiration Date: |
| ☐ Acknowledgment | ☐ Driver's License | |
| ☐ Other: | ☐ Other: | |

| | | |
|---|---|---|
| Witness Full Name: | Phone Number: | |
| Email Address: | Witness Signature: | Thumbprint: |
| Address: | | |
| Document Type: | Date/Time Notarized: | Document Date: |
| Comments: | | |

## NOTARY LOG

| Full Name | Phone Number: | Record Number: **169** |
|---|---|---|
| Email Address: | Signer's Signature: | $ Amount charged: |
| Address: | | Method of Payment: |
| | Gas & Mileage: | ☐ Cash ☐ Credit ☐ Check |

| Notary Service(s) Provided: | Identification: | ID Number: |
|---|---|---|
| ☐ Jurat | ☐ ID Card ☐ Credible Witness | Issued By: |
| ☐ Oath/Affirmations | ☐ Passport ☐ Known Personally | Date Issued: | Expiration Date: |
| ☐ Acknowledgment | ☐ Driver's License | |
| ☐ Other: | ☐ Other: | |

| Witness Full Name: | Phone Number: | |
|---|---|---|
| Email Address: | Witness Signature: | Thumbprint: |
| Address: | | |

| Document Type: | Date/Time Notarized: | Document Date: |
|---|---|---|
| Comments: | | |

---

## NOTARY LOG

| Full Name | Phone Number: | Record Number: **170** |
|---|---|---|
| Email Address: | Signer's Signature: | $ Amount charged: |
| Address: | | Method of Payment: |
| | Gas & Mileage: | ☐ Cash ☐ Credit ☐ Check |

| Notary Service(s) Provided: | Identification: | ID Number: |
|---|---|---|
| ☐ Jurat | ☐ ID Card ☐ Credible Witness | Issued By: |
| ☐ Oath/Affirmations | ☐ Passport ☐ Known Personally | Date Issued: | Expiration Date: |
| ☐ Acknowledgment | ☐ Driver's License | |
| ☐ Other: | ☐ Other: | |

| Witness Full Name: | Phone Number: | |
|---|---|---|
| Email Address: | Witness Signature: | Thumbprint: |
| Address: | | |

| Document Type: | Date/Time Notarized: | Document Date: |
|---|---|---|
| Comments: | | |

## NOTARY LOG

| Full Name | Phone Number: | Record Number: **171** |
|---|---|---|
| Email Address: | Signer's Signature: | $ Amount charged: |
| Address: | | Method of Payment: |
| | Gas & Mileage: | ☐ Cash   ☐ Credit   ☐ Check |

| Notary Service(s) Provided: | Identification: | ID Number: |
|---|---|---|
| ☐ Jurat | ☐ ID Card   ☐ Credible Witness | Issued By: |
| ☐ Oath/Affirmations | ☐ Passport   ☐ Known Personally | Date Issued:   Expiration Date: |
| ☐ Acknowledgment | ☐ Driver's License | |
| ☐ Other: | ☐ Other: | |

| Witness Full Name: | Phone Number: | |
|---|---|---|
| Email Address: | Witness Signature: | Thumbprint: |
| Address: | | |

| Document Type: | Date/Time Notarized: | Document Date: |
|---|---|---|

Comments:

---

## NOTARY LOG

| Full Name | Phone Number: | Record Number: **172** |
|---|---|---|
| Email Address: | Signer's Signature: | $ Amount charged: |
| Address: | | Method of Payment: |
| | Gas & Mileage: | ☐ Cash   ☐ Credit   ☐ Check |

| Notary Service(s) Provided: | Identification: | ID Number: |
|---|---|---|
| ☐ Jurat | ☐ ID Card   ☐ Credible Witness | Issued By: |
| ☐ Oath/Affirmations | ☐ Passport   ☐ Known Personally | Date Issued:   Expiration Date: |
| ☐ Acknowledgment | ☐ Driver's License | |
| ☐ Other: | ☐ Other: | |

| Witness Full Name: | Phone Number: | |
|---|---|---|
| Email Address: | Witness Signature: | Thumbprint: |
| Address: | | |

| Document Type: | Date/Time Notarized: | Document Date: |
|---|---|---|

Comments:

## NOTARY LOG

| | | |
|---|---|---|
| Full Name | Phone Number: | Record Number: **173** |
| Email Address: | Signer's Signature: | $ Amount charged: |
| Address: | | Method of Payment: |
| | Gas & Mileage: | ☐ Cash  ☐ Credit  ☐ Check |
| Notary Service(s) Provided: | Identification: | ID Number: |
| ☐ Jurat | ☐ ID Card   ☐ Credible Witness | Issued By: |
| ☐ Oath/Affirmations | ☐ Passport   ☐ Known Personally | Date Issued:   Expiration Date: |
| ☐ Acknowledgment | ☐ Driver's License | |
| ☐ Other: | ☐ Other: | |
| Witness Full Name: | Phone Number: | |
| Email Address: | Witness Signature: | Thumbprint: |
| Address: | | |
| Document Type: | Date/Time Notarized: | Document Date: |
| Comments: | | |

## NOTARY LOG

| | | |
|---|---|---|
| Full Name | Phone Number: | Record Number: **174** |
| Email Address: | Signer's Signature: | $ Amount charged: |
| Address: | | Method of Payment: |
| | Gas & Mileage: | ☐ Cash  ☐ Credit  ☐ Check |
| Notary Service(s) Provided: | Identification: | ID Number: |
| ☐ Jurat | ☐ ID Card   ☐ Credible Witness | Issued By: |
| ☐ Oath/Affirmations | ☐ Passport   ☐ Known Personally | Date Issued:   Expiration Date: |
| ☐ Acknowledgment | ☐ Driver's License | |
| ☐ Other: | ☐ Other: | |
| Witness Full Name: | Phone Number: | |
| Email Address: | Witness Signature: | Thumbprint: |
| Address: | | |
| Document Type: | Date/Time Notarized: | Document Date: |
| Comments: | | |

## NOTARY LOG

| Full Name | Phone Number: | Record Number: **175** |
|---|---|---|
| Email Address: | Signer's Signature: | $ Amount charged: |
| Address: | | Method of Payment: |
| | Gas & Mileage: | ☐ Cash   ☐ Credit   ☐ Check |

| Notary Service(s) Provided: | Identification: | ID Number: |
|---|---|---|
| ☐ Jurat | ☐ ID Card    ☐ Credible Witness | Issued By: |
| ☐ Oath/Affirmations | ☐ Passport    ☐ Known Personally | Date Issued:    Expiration Date: |
| ☐ Acknowledgment | ☐ Driver's License | |
| ☐ Other: | ☐ Other: | |

| Witness Full Name: | Phone Number: | |
|---|---|---|
| Email Address: | Witness Signature: | Thumbprint: |
| Address: | | |

| Document Type: | Date/Time Notarized: | Document Date: |
|---|---|---|

Comments:

---

## NOTARY LOG

| Full Name | Phone Number: | Record Number: **176** |
|---|---|---|
| Email Address: | Signer's Signature: | $ Amount charged: |
| Address: | | Method of Payment: |
| | Gas & Mileage: | ☐ Cash   ☐ Credit   ☐ Check |

| Notary Service(s) Provided: | Identification: | ID Number: |
|---|---|---|
| ☐ Jurat | ☐ ID Card    ☐ Credible Witness | Issued By: |
| ☐ Oath/Affirmations | ☐ Passport    ☐ Known Personally | Date Issued:    Expiration Date: |
| ☐ Acknowledgment | ☐ Driver's License | |
| ☐ Other: | ☐ Other: | |

| Witness Full Name: | Phone Number: | |
|---|---|---|
| Email Address: | Witness Signature: | Thumbprint: |
| Address: | | |

| Document Type: | Date/Time Notarized: | Document Date: |
|---|---|---|

Comments:

## NOTARY LOG

| Full Name | Phone Number: | Record Number: **177** |
|---|---|---|
| Email Address: | Signer's Signature: | $ Amount charged: |
| Address: | | Method of Payment: |
| | Gas & Mileage: | ☐ Cash  ☐ Credit  ☐ Check |

| Notary Service(s) Provided: | Identification: | | ID Number: | |
|---|---|---|---|---|
| ☐ Jurat | ☐ ID Card | ☐ Credible Witness | Issued By: | |
| ☐ Oath/Affirmations | ☐ Passport | ☐ Known Personally | Date Issued: | Expiration Date: |
| ☐ Acknowledgment | ☐ Driver's License | | | |
| ☐ Other: | ☐ Other: | | | |

| Witness Full Name: | Phone Number: | |
|---|---|---|
| Email Address: | Witness Signature: | Thumbprint: |
| Address: | | |

| Document Type: | Date/Time Notarized: | Document Date: | |
|---|---|---|---|
| Comments: | | | |

---

## NOTARY LOG

| Full Name | Phone Number: | Record Number: **178** |
|---|---|---|
| Email Address: | Signer's Signature: | $ Amount charged: |
| Address: | | Method of Payment: |
| | Gas & Mileage: | ☐ Cash  ☐ Credit  ☐ Check |

| Notary Service(s) Provided: | Identification: | | ID Number: | |
|---|---|---|---|---|
| ☐ Jurat | ☐ ID Card | ☐ Credible Witness | Issued By: | |
| ☐ Oath/Affirmations | ☐ Passport | ☐ Known Personally | Date Issued: | Expiration Date: |
| ☐ Acknowledgment | ☐ Driver's License | | | |
| ☐ Other: | ☐ Other: | | | |

| Witness Full Name: | Phone Number: | |
|---|---|---|
| Email Address: | Witness Signature: | Thumbprint: |
| Address: | | |

| Document Type: | Date/Time Notarized: | Document Date: | |
|---|---|---|---|
| Comments: | | | |

## NOTARY LOG

| Full Name | Phone Number: | Record Number: **179** |
|---|---|---|
| Email Address: | Signer's Signature: | $ Amount charged: |
| Address: | | Method of Payment: |
| | Gas & Mileage: | ☐ Cash   ☐ Credit   ☐ Check |

| Notary Service(s) Provided: | Identification: | ID Number: |
|---|---|---|
| ☐ Jurat | ☐ ID Card   ☐ Credible Witness | Issued By: |
| ☐ Oath/Affirmations | ☐ Passport   ☐ Known Personally | Date Issued:   Expiration Date: |
| ☐ Acknowledgment | ☐ Driver's License | |
| ☐ Other: | ☐ Other: | |

| Witness Full Name: | Phone Number: | |
|---|---|---|
| Email Address: | Witness Signature: | Thumbprint: |
| Address: | | |

| Document Type: | Date/Time Notarized: | Document Date: |
|---|---|---|
| Comments: | | |

## NOTARY LOG

| Full Name | Phone Number: | Record Number: **180** |
|---|---|---|
| Email Address: | Signer's Signature: | $ Amount charged: |
| Address: | | Method of Payment: |
| | Gas & Mileage: | ☐ Cash   ☐ Credit   ☐ Check |

| Notary Service(s) Provided: | Identification: | ID Number: |
|---|---|---|
| ☐ Jurat | ☐ ID Card   ☐ Credible Witness | Issued By: |
| ☐ Oath/Affirmations | ☐ Passport   ☐ Known Personally | Date Issued:   Expiration Date: |
| ☐ Acknowledgment | ☐ Driver's License | |
| ☐ Other: | ☐ Other: | |

| Witness Full Name: | Phone Number: | |
|---|---|---|
| Email Address: | Witness Signature: | Thumbprint: |
| Address: | | |

| Document Type: | Date/Time Notarized: | Document Date: |
|---|---|---|
| Comments: | | |

## NOTARY LOG

| | | |
|---|---|---|
| Full Name | Phone Number: | Record Number: **181** |
| Email Address: | Signer's Signature: | $ Amount charged: |
| Address: | | Method of Payment: |
| | Gas & Mileage: | ☐ Cash  ☐ Credit  ☐ Check |
| Notary Service(s) Provided: | Identification: | ID Number: |
| ☐ Jurat | ☐ ID Card   ☐ Credible Witness | Issued By: |
| ☐ Oath/Affirmations | ☐ Passport   ☐ Known Personally | Date Issued:   Expiration Date: |
| ☐ Acknowledgment | ☐ Driver's License | |
| ☐ Other: | ☐ Other: | |

| | | |
|---|---|---|
| Witness Full Name: | Phone Number: | |
| Email Address: | Witness Signature: | Thumbprint: |
| Address: | | |
| Document Type: | Date/Time Notarized:   Document Date: | |
| Comments: | | |

## NOTARY LOG

| | | |
|---|---|---|
| Full Name | Phone Number: | Record Number: **182** |
| Email Address: | Signer's Signature: | $ Amount charged: |
| Address: | | Method of Payment: |
| | Gas & Mileage: | ☐ Cash  ☐ Credit  ☐ Check |
| Notary Service(s) Provided: | Identification: | ID Number: |
| ☐ Jurat | ☐ ID Card   ☐ Credible Witness | Issued By: |
| ☐ Oath/Affirmations | ☐ Passport   ☐ Known Personally | Date Issued:   Expiration Date: |
| ☐ Acknowledgment | ☐ Driver's License | |
| ☐ Other: | ☐ Other: | |

| | | |
|---|---|---|
| Witness Full Name: | Phone Number: | |
| Email Address: | Witness Signature: | Thumbprint: |
| Address: | | |
| Document Type: | Date/Time Notarized:   Document Date: | |
| Comments: | | |

## NOTARY LOG

| Full Name | Phone Number: | Record Number: **183** |
|---|---|---|
| Email Address: | Signer's Signature: | $ Amount charged: |
| Address: | | Method of Payment: |
| | Gas & Mileage: | ☐ Cash  ☐ Credit  ☐ Check |

| Notary Service(s) Provided: | Identification: | ID Number: |
|---|---|---|
| ☐ Jurat | ☐ ID Card   ☐ Credible Witness | Issued By: |
| ☐ Oath/Affirmations | ☐ Passport   ☐ Known Personally | Date Issued:   Expiration Date: |
| ☐ Acknowledgment | ☐ Driver's License | |
| ☐ Other: | ☐ Other: | |

| Witness Full Name: | Phone Number: | |
|---|---|---|
| Email Address: | Witness Signature: | Thumbprint: |
| Address: | | |

| Document Type: | Date/Time Notarized: | Document Date: |
|---|---|---|
| Comments: | | |

## NOTARY LOG

| Full Name | Phone Number: | Record Number: **184** |
|---|---|---|
| Email Address: | Signer's Signature: | $ Amount charged: |
| Address: | | Method of Payment: |
| | Gas & Mileage: | ☐ Cash  ☐ Credit  ☐ Check |

| Notary Service(s) Provided: | Identification: | ID Number: |
|---|---|---|
| ☐ Jurat | ☐ ID Card   ☐ Credible Witness | Issued By: |
| ☐ Oath/Affirmations | ☐ Passport   ☐ Known Personally | Date Issued:   Expiration Date: |
| ☐ Acknowledgment | ☐ Driver's License | |
| ☐ Other: | ☐ Other: | |

| Witness Full Name: | Phone Number: | |
|---|---|---|
| Email Address: | Witness Signature: | Thumbprint: |
| Address: | | |

| Document Type: | Date/Time Notarized: | Document Date: |
|---|---|---|
| Comments: | | |

## NOTARY LOG

| Full Name | Phone Number: | Record Number: **185** |
|---|---|---|
| Email Address: | Signer's Signature: | $ Amount charged: |
| Address: | | Method of Payment: |
| | Gas & Mileage: | ☐ Cash   ☐ Credit   ☐ Check |

| Notary Service(s) Provided: | Identification: | ID Number: |
|---|---|---|
| ☐ Jurat | ☐ ID Card   ☐ Credible Witness | Issued By: |
| ☐ Oath/Affirmations | ☐ Passport   ☐ Known Personally | Date Issued:   Expiration Date: |
| ☐ Acknowledgment | ☐ Driver's License | |
| ☐ Other: | ☐ Other: | |

| Witness Full Name: | Phone Number: | |
|---|---|---|
| Email Address: | Witness Signature: | Thumbprint: |
| Address: | | |

| Document Type: | Date/Time Notarized: | Document Date: |
|---|---|---|
| Comments: | | |

## NOTARY LOG

| Full Name | Phone Number: | Record Number: **186** |
|---|---|---|
| Email Address: | Signer's Signature: | $ Amount charged: |
| Address: | | Method of Payment: |
| | Gas & Mileage: | ☐ Cash   ☐ Credit   ☐ Check |

| Notary Service(s) Provided: | Identification: | ID Number: |
|---|---|---|
| ☐ Jurat | ☐ ID Card   ☐ Credible Witness | Issued By: |
| ☐ Oath/Affirmations | ☐ Passport   ☐ Known Personally | Date Issued:   Expiration Date: |
| ☐ Acknowledgment | ☐ Driver's License | |
| ☐ Other: | ☐ Other: | |

| Witness Full Name: | Phone Number: | |
|---|---|---|
| Email Address: | Witness Signature: | Thumbprint: |
| Address: | | |

| Document Type: | Date/Time Notarized: | Document Date: |
|---|---|---|
| Comments: | | |

## NOTARY LOG

| Full Name | Phone Number: | Record Number: **187** |
|---|---|---|
| Email Address: | Signer's Signature: | $ Amount charged: |
| Address: | | Method of Payment: |
| | Gas & Mileage: | ☐ Cash    ☐ Credit    ☐ Check |

| Notary Service(s) Provided: | Identification: | ID Number: |
|---|---|---|
| ☐ Jurat | ☐ ID Card    ☐ Credible Witness | Issued By: |
| ☐ Oath/Affirmations | ☐ Passport    ☐ Known Personally | Date Issued: | Expiration Date: |
| ☐ Acknowledgment | ☐ Driver's License | | |
| ☐ Other: | ☐ Other: | | |

| Witness Full Name: | Phone Number: | |
|---|---|---|
| Email Address: | Witness Signature: | Thumbprint: |
| Address: | | |

| Document Type: | Date/Time Notarized: | Document Date: |
|---|---|---|
| Comments: | | |

## NOTARY LOG

| Full Name | Phone Number: | Record Number: **188** |
|---|---|---|
| Email Address: | Signer's Signature: | $ Amount charged: |
| Address: | | Method of Payment: |
| | Gas & Mileage: | ☐ Cash    ☐ Credit    ☐ Check |

| Notary Service(s) Provided: | Identification: | ID Number: |
|---|---|---|
| ☐ Jurat | ☐ ID Card    ☐ Credible Witness | Issued By: |
| ☐ Oath/Affirmations | ☐ Passport    ☐ Known Personally | Date Issued: | Expiration Date: |
| ☐ Acknowledgment | ☐ Driver's License | | |
| ☐ Other: | ☐ Other: | | |

| Witness Full Name: | Phone Number: | |
|---|---|---|
| Email Address: | Witness Signature: | Thumbprint: |
| Address: | | |

| Document Type: | Date/Time Notarized: | Document Date: |
|---|---|---|
| Comments: | | |

## NOTARY LOG

| Full Name | Phone Number: | Record Number: **189** |
|---|---|---|
| Email Address: | Signer's Signature: | $ Amount charged: |
| Address: | | Method of Payment: |
| | Gas & Mileage: | ☐ Cash  ☐ Credit  ☐ Check |

| Notary Service(s) Provided: | Identification: | ID Number: |
|---|---|---|
| ☐ Jurat | ☐ ID Card  ☐ Credible Witness | Issued By: |
| ☐ Oath/Affirmations | ☐ Passport  ☐ Known Personally | Date Issued:   Expiration Date: |
| ☐ Acknowledgment | ☐ Driver's License | |
| ☐ Other: | ☐ Other: | |

| Witness Full Name: | Phone Number: | |
|---|---|---|
| Email Address: | Witness Signature: | Thumbprint: |
| Address: | | |

| Document Type: | Date/Time Notarized: | Document Date: |
|---|---|---|

Comments:

---

## NOTARY LOG

| Full Name | Phone Number: | Record Number: **190** |
|---|---|---|
| Email Address: | Signer's Signature: | $ Amount charged: |
| Address: | | Method of Payment: |
| | Gas & Mileage: | ☐ Cash  ☐ Credit  ☐ Check |

| Notary Service(s) Provided: | Identification: | ID Number: |
|---|---|---|
| ☐ Jurat | ☐ ID Card  ☐ Credible Witness | Issued By: |
| ☐ Oath/Affirmations | ☐ Passport  ☐ Known Personally | Date Issued:   Expiration Date: |
| ☐ Acknowledgment | ☐ Driver's License | |
| ☐ Other: | ☐ Other: | |

| Witness Full Name: | Phone Number: | |
|---|---|---|
| Email Address: | Witness Signature: | Thumbprint: |
| Address: | | |

| Document Type: | Date/Time Notarized: | Document Date: |
|---|---|---|

Comments:

## NOTARY LOG

| Full Name | Phone Number: | Record Number: **191** |
|---|---|---|
| Email Address: | Signer's Signature: | $ Amount charged: |
| Address: | | Method of Payment: |
| | Gas & Mileage: | ☐ Cash  ☐ Credit  ☐ Check |

| Notary Service(s) Provided: | Identification: | ID Number: |
|---|---|---|
| ☐ Jurat | ☐ ID Card    ☐ Credible Witness | Issued By: |
| ☐ Oath/Affirmations | ☐ Passport    ☐ Known Personally | Date Issued:    Expiration Date: |
| ☐ Acknowledgment | ☐ Driver's License | |
| ☐ Other: | ☐ Other: | |

| Witness Full Name: | Phone Number: | |
|---|---|---|
| Email Address: | Witness Signature: | Thumbprint: |
| Address: | | |

| Document Type: | Date/Time Notarized: | Document Date: |
|---|---|---|

Comments:

---

## NOTARY LOG

| Full Name | Phone Number: | Record Number: **192** |
|---|---|---|
| Email Address: | Signer's Signature: | $ Amount charged: |
| Address: | | Method of Payment: |
| | Gas & Mileage: | ☐ Cash  ☐ Credit  ☐ Check |

| Notary Service(s) Provided: | Identification: | ID Number: |
|---|---|---|
| ☐ Jurat | ☐ ID Card    ☐ Credible Witness | Issued By: |
| ☐ Oath/Affirmations | ☐ Passport    ☐ Known Personally | Date Issued:    Expiration Date: |
| ☐ Acknowledgment | ☐ Driver's License | |
| ☐ Other: | ☐ Other: | |

| Witness Full Name: | Phone Number: | |
|---|---|---|
| Email Address: | Witness Signature: | Thumbprint: |
| Address: | | |

| Document Type: | Date/Time Notarized: | Document Date: |
|---|---|---|

Comments:

## NOTARY LOG

| Full Name | Phone Number: | Record Number: **193** |
|---|---|---|
| Email Address: | Signer's Signature: | $ Amount charged: |
| Address: | | Method of Payment: |
| | Gas & Mileage: | ☐ Cash ☐ Credit ☐ Check |

| Notary Service(s) Provided: | Identification: | ID Number: |
|---|---|---|
| ☐ Jurat | ☐ ID Card ☐ Credible Witness | Issued By: |
| ☐ Oath/Affirmations | ☐ Passport ☐ Known Personally | Date Issued: / Expiration Date: |
| ☐ Acknowledgment | ☐ Driver's License | |
| ☐ Other: | ☐ Other: | |

| Witness Full Name: | Phone Number: | |
|---|---|---|
| Email Address: | Witness Signature: | Thumbprint: |
| Address: | | |

| Document Type: | Date/Time Notarized: | Document Date: |
|---|---|---|

Comments:

---

## NOTARY LOG

| Full Name | Phone Number: | Record Number: **194** |
|---|---|---|
| Email Address: | Signer's Signature: | $ Amount charged: |
| Address: | | Method of Payment: |
| | Gas & Mileage: | ☐ Cash ☐ Credit ☐ Check |

| Notary Service(s) Provided: | Identification: | ID Number: |
|---|---|---|
| ☐ Jurat | ☐ ID Card ☐ Credible Witness | Issued By: |
| ☐ Oath/Affirmations | ☐ Passport ☐ Known Personally | Date Issued: / Expiration Date: |
| ☐ Acknowledgment | ☐ Driver's License | |
| ☐ Other: | ☐ Other: | |

| Witness Full Name: | Phone Number: | |
|---|---|---|
| Email Address: | Witness Signature: | Thumbprint: |
| Address: | | |

| Document Type: | Date/Time Notarized: | Document Date: |
|---|---|---|

Comments:

## NOTARY LOG

| Full Name | Phone Number: | Record Number: **195** |
|---|---|---|
| Email Address: | Signer's Signature: | $ Amount charged: |
| Address: | | Method of Payment: |
| | Gas & Mileage: | ☐ Cash   ☐ Credit   ☐ Check |

| Notary Service(s) Provided: | Identification: | ID Number: |
|---|---|---|
| ☐ Jurat | ☐ ID Card   ☐ Credible Witness | Issued By: |
| ☐ Oath/Affirmations | ☐ Passport   ☐ Known Personally | Date Issued:   Expiration Date: |
| ☐ Acknowledgment | ☐ Driver's License | |
| ☐ Other: | ☐ Other: | |

| Witness Full Name: | Phone Number: | |
|---|---|---|
| Email Address: | Witness Signature: | Thumbprint: |
| Address: | | |

| Document Type: | Date/Time Notarized: | Document Date: |
|---|---|---|

Comments:

---

## NOTARY LOG

| Full Name | Phone Number: | Record Number: **196** |
|---|---|---|
| Email Address: | Signer's Signature: | $ Amount charged: |
| Address: | | Method of Payment: |
| | Gas & Mileage: | ☐ Cash   ☐ Credit   ☐ Check |

| Notary Service(s) Provided: | Identification: | ID Number: |
|---|---|---|
| ☐ Jurat | ☐ ID Card   ☐ Credible Witness | Issued By: |
| ☐ Oath/Affirmations | ☐ Passport   ☐ Known Personally | Date Issued:   Expiration Date: |
| ☐ Acknowledgment | ☐ Driver's License | |
| ☐ Other: | ☐ Other: | |

| Witness Full Name: | Phone Number: | |
|---|---|---|
| Email Address: | Witness Signature: | Thumbprint: |
| Address: | | |

| Document Type: | Date/Time Notarized: | Document Date: |
|---|---|---|

Comments:

## NOTARY LOG

| Full Name | Phone Number: | Record Number: **197** |
|---|---|---|
| Email Address: | Signer's Signature: | $ Amount charged: |
| Address: | | Method of Payment: |
| | Gas & Mileage: | ☐ Cash ☐ Credit ☐ Check |

| Notary Service(s) Provided: | Identification: | ID Number: |
|---|---|---|
| ☐ Jurat | ☐ ID Card ☐ Credible Witness | Issued By: |
| ☐ Oath/Affirmations | ☐ Passport ☐ Known Personally | Date Issued: / Expiration Date: |
| ☐ Acknowledgment | ☐ Driver's License | |
| ☐ Other: | ☐ Other: | |

| Witness Full Name: | Phone Number: | |
|---|---|---|
| Email Address: | Witness Signature: | Thumbprint: |
| Address: | | |

| Document Type: | Date/Time Notarized: | Document Date: |
|---|---|---|
| Comments: | | |

---

## NOTARY LOG

| Full Name | Phone Number: | Record Number: **198** |
|---|---|---|
| Email Address: | Signer's Signature: | $ Amount charged: |
| Address: | | Method of Payment: |
| | Gas & Mileage: | ☐ Cash ☐ Credit ☐ Check |

| Notary Service(s) Provided: | Identification: | ID Number: |
|---|---|---|
| ☐ Jurat | ☐ ID Card ☐ Credible Witness | Issued By: |
| ☐ Oath/Affirmations | ☐ Passport ☐ Known Personally | Date Issued: / Expiration Date: |
| ☐ Acknowledgment | ☐ Driver's License | |
| ☐ Other: | ☐ Other: | |

| Witness Full Name: | Phone Number: | |
|---|---|---|
| Email Address: | Witness Signature: | Thumbprint: |
| Address: | | |

| Document Type: | Date/Time Notarized: | Document Date: |
|---|---|---|
| Comments: | | |

## NOTARY LOG

| | | |
|---|---|---|
| Full Name | Phone Number: | Record Number: **199** |
| Email Address: | Signer's Signature: | $ Amount charged: |
| Address: | | Method of Payment: |
| | Gas & Mileage: | ☐ Cash   ☐ Credit   ☐ Check |
| Notary Service(s) Provided: | Identification: | ID Number: |
| ☐ Jurat | ☐ ID Card   ☐ Credible Witness | Issued By: |
| ☐ Oath/Affirmations | ☐ Passport   ☐ Known Personally | Date Issued:   Expiration Date: |
| ☐ Acknowledgment | ☐ Driver's License | |
| ☐ Other: | ☐ Other: | |

| | |
|---|---|
| Witness Full Name: | Phone Number: |
| Email Address: | Witness Signature:   Thumbprint: |
| Address: | |
| Document Type:   Date/Time Notarized: | Document Date: |
| Comments: | |

## NOTARY LOG

| | | |
|---|---|---|
| Full Name | Phone Number: | Record Number: **200** |
| Email Address: | Signer's Signature: | $ Amount charged: |
| Address: | | Method of Payment: |
| | Gas & Mileage: | ☐ Cash   ☐ Credit   ☐ Check |
| Notary Service(s) Provided: | Identification: | ID Number: |
| ☐ Jurat | ☐ ID Card   ☐ Credible Witness | Issued By: |
| ☐ Oath/Affirmations | ☐ Passport   ☐ Known Personally | Date Issued:   Expiration Date: |
| ☐ Acknowledgment | ☐ Driver's License | |
| ☐ Other: | ☐ Other: | |

| | |
|---|---|
| Witness Full Name: | Phone Number: |
| Email Address: | Witness Signature:   Thumbprint: |
| Address: | |
| Document Type:   Date/Time Notarized: | Document Date: |
| Comments: | |

## NOTARY LOG

| Full Name | Phone Number: | Record Number: **201** |
|---|---|---|
| Email Address: | Signer's Signature: | $ Amount charged: |
| Address: | | Method of Payment: |
| | Gas & Mileage: | ☐ Cash   ☐ Credit   ☐ Check |

| Notary Service(s) Provided: | Identification: | ID Number: | |
|---|---|---|---|
| ☐ Jurat | ☐ ID Card   ☐ Credible Witness | Issued By: | |
| ☐ Oath/Affirmations | ☐ Passport   ☐ Known Personally | Date Issued: | Expiration Date: |
| ☐ Acknowledgment | ☐ Driver's License | | |
| ☐ Other: | ☐ Other: | | |

| Witness Full Name: | Phone Number: | |
|---|---|---|
| Email Address: | Witness Signature: | Thumbprint: |
| Address: | | |

| Document Type: | Date/Time Notarized: | Document Date: |
|---|---|---|
| Comments: | | |

## NOTARY LOG

| Full Name | Phone Number: | Record Number: **202** |
|---|---|---|
| Email Address: | Signer's Signature: | $ Amount charged: |
| Address: | | Method of Payment: |
| | Gas & Mileage: | ☐ Cash   ☐ Credit   ☐ Check |

| Notary Service(s) Provided: | Identification: | ID Number: | |
|---|---|---|---|
| ☐ Jurat | ☐ ID Card   ☐ Credible Witness | Issued By: | |
| ☐ Oath/Affirmations | ☐ Passport   ☐ Known Personally | Date Issued: | Expiration Date: |
| ☐ Acknowledgment | ☐ Driver's License | | |
| ☐ Other: | ☐ Other: | | |

| Witness Full Name: | Phone Number: | |
|---|---|---|
| Email Address: | Witness Signature: | Thumbprint: |
| Address: | | |

| Document Type: | Date/Time Notarized: | Document Date: |
|---|---|---|
| Comments: | | |

## NOTARY LOG

| Full Name | Phone Number: | Record Number: **203** |
|---|---|---|
| Email Address: | Signer's Signature: | $ Amount charged: |
| Address: | | Method of Payment: |
| | Gas & Mileage: | ☐ Cash   ☐ Credit   ☐ Check |

| Notary Service(s) Provided: | Identification: | ID Number: |
|---|---|---|
| ☐ Jurat | ☐ ID Card   ☐ Credible Witness | Issued By: |
| ☐ Oath/Affirmations | ☐ Passport   ☐ Known Personally | Date Issued:   Expiration Date: |
| ☐ Acknowledgment | ☐ Driver's License | |
| ☐ Other: | ☐ Other: | |

| Witness Full Name: | Phone Number: | |
|---|---|---|
| Email Address: | Witness Signature: | Thumbprint: |
| Address: | | |

| Document Type: | Date/Time Notarized: | Document Date: |
|---|---|---|

Comments:

---

## NOTARY LOG

| Full Name | Phone Number: | Record Number: **204** |
|---|---|---|
| Email Address: | Signer's Signature: | $ Amount charged: |
| Address: | | Method of Payment: |
| | Gas & Mileage: | ☐ Cash   ☐ Credit   ☐ Check |

| Notary Service(s) Provided: | Identification: | ID Number: |
|---|---|---|
| ☐ Jurat | ☐ ID Card   ☐ Credible Witness | Issued By: |
| ☐ Oath/Affirmations | ☐ Passport   ☐ Known Personally | Date Issued:   Expiration Date: |
| ☐ Acknowledgment | ☐ Driver's License | |
| ☐ Other: | ☐ Other: | |

| Witness Full Name: | Phone Number: | |
|---|---|---|
| Email Address: | Witness Signature: | Thumbprint: |
| Address: | | |

| Document Type: | Date/Time Notarized: | Document Date: |
|---|---|---|

Comments:

## NOTARY LOG

| Full Name | Phone Number: | Record Number: **205** |
|---|---|---|
| Email Address: | Signer's Signature: | $ Amount charged: |
| Address: | | Method of Payment: |
| | Gas & Mileage: | ☐ Cash  ☐ Credit  ☐ Check |

| Notary Service(s) Provided: | Identification: | ID Number: |
|---|---|---|
| ☐ Jurat | ☐ ID Card   ☐ Credible Witness | Issued By: |
| ☐ Oath/Affirmations | ☐ Passport   ☐ Known Personally | Date Issued:   Expiration Date: |
| ☐ Acknowledgment | ☐ Driver's License | |
| ☐ Other: | ☐ Other: | |

| Witness Full Name: | Phone Number: | |
|---|---|---|
| Email Address: | Witness Signature: | Thumbprint: |
| Address: | | |

| Document Type: | Date/Time Notarized: | Document Date: |
|---|---|---|

Comments:

---

## NOTARY LOG

| Full Name | Phone Number: | Record Number: **206** |
|---|---|---|
| Email Address: | Signer's Signature: | $ Amount charged: |
| Address: | | Method of Payment: |
| | Gas & Mileage: | ☐ Cash  ☐ Credit  ☐ Check |

| Notary Service(s) Provided: | Identification: | ID Number: |
|---|---|---|
| ☐ Jurat | ☐ ID Card   ☐ Credible Witness | Issued By: |
| ☐ Oath/Affirmations | ☐ Passport   ☐ Known Personally | Date Issued:   Expiration Date: |
| ☐ Acknowledgment | ☐ Driver's License | |
| ☐ Other: | ☐ Other: | |

| Witness Full Name: | Phone Number: | |
|---|---|---|
| Email Address: | Witness Signature: | Thumbprint: |
| Address: | | |

| Document Type: | Date/Time Notarized: | Document Date: |
|---|---|---|

Comments:

## NOTARY LOG

| Full Name | Phone Number: | Record Number: **207** |
|---|---|---|
| Email Address: | Signer's Signature: | $ Amount charged: |
| Address: | | Method of Payment: |
| | Gas & Mileage: | ☐ Cash  ☐ Credit  ☐ Check |

| Notary Service(s) Provided: | Identification: | ID Number: |
|---|---|---|
| ☐ Jurat | ☐ ID Card   ☐ Credible Witness | Issued By: |
| ☐ Oath/Affirmations | ☐ Passport   ☐ Known Personally | Date Issued: | Expiration Date: |
| ☐ Acknowledgment | ☐ Driver's License | |
| ☐ Other: | ☐ Other: | |

| Witness Full Name: | Phone Number: | |
|---|---|---|
| Email Address: | Witness Signature: | Thumbprint: |
| Address: | | |

| Document Type: | Date/Time Notarized: | Document Date: |
|---|---|---|
| Comments: | | |

---

## NOTARY LOG

| Full Name | Phone Number: | Record Number: **208** |
|---|---|---|
| Email Address: | Signer's Signature: | $ Amount charged: |
| Address: | | Method of Payment: |
| | Gas & Mileage: | ☐ Cash  ☐ Credit  ☐ Check |

| Notary Service(s) Provided: | Identification: | ID Number: |
|---|---|---|
| ☐ Jurat | ☐ ID Card   ☐ Credible Witness | Issued By: |
| ☐ Oath/Affirmations | ☐ Passport   ☐ Known Personally | Date Issued: | Expiration Date: |
| ☐ Acknowledgment | ☐ Driver's License | |
| ☐ Other: | ☐ Other: | |

| Witness Full Name: | Phone Number: | |
|---|---|---|
| Email Address: | Witness Signature: | Thumbprint: |
| Address: | | |

| Document Type: | Date/Time Notarized: | Document Date: |
|---|---|---|
| Comments: | | |

# NOTARY LOG

| Full Name | Phone Number: | Record Number: **209** |
|---|---|---|
| Email Address: | Signer's Signature: | $ Amount charged: |
| Address: | | Method of Payment: |
| | Gas & Mileage: | ☐ Cash   ☐ Credit   ☐ Check |

| Notary Service(s) Provided: | Identification: | ID Number: |
|---|---|---|
| ☐ Jurat | ☐ ID Card   ☐ Credible Witness | Issued By: |
| ☐ Oath/Affirmations | ☐ Passport   ☐ Known Personally | Date Issued:   Expiration Date: |
| ☐ Acknowledgment | ☐ Driver's License | |
| ☐ Other: | ☐ Other: | |

| Witness Full Name: | Phone Number: | |
|---|---|---|
| Email Address: | Witness Signature: | Thumbprint: |
| Address: | | |

| Document Type: | Date/Time Notarized: | Document Date: |
|---|---|---|
| Comments: | | |

# NOTARY LOG

| Full Name | Phone Number: | Record Number: **210** |
|---|---|---|
| Email Address: | Signer's Signature: | $ Amount charged: |
| Address: | | Method of Payment: |
| | Gas & Mileage: | ☐ Cash   ☐ Credit   ☐ Check |

| Notary Service(s) Provided: | Identification: | ID Number: |
|---|---|---|
| ☐ Jurat | ☐ ID Card   ☐ Credible Witness | Issued By: |
| ☐ Oath/Affirmations | ☐ Passport   ☐ Known Personally | Date Issued:   Expiration Date: |
| ☐ Acknowledgment | ☐ Driver's License | |
| ☐ Other: | ☐ Other: | |

| Witness Full Name: | Phone Number: | |
|---|---|---|
| Email Address: | Witness Signature: | Thumbprint: |
| Address: | | |

| Document Type: | Date/Time Notarized: | Document Date: |
|---|---|---|
| Comments: | | |

## NOTARY LOG

| | | |
|---|---|---|
| Full Name | Phone Number: | Record Number: **211** |
| Email Address: | Signer's Signature: | $ Amount charged: |
| Address: | | Method of Payment: |
| | Gas & Mileage: | ☐ Cash  ☐ Credit  ☐ Check |
| Notary Service(s) Provided: | Identification: | ID Number: |
| ☐ Jurat | ☐ ID Card  ☐ Credible Witness | Issued By: |
| ☐ Oath/Affirmations | ☐ Passport  ☐ Known Personally | Date Issued: | Expiration Date: |
| ☐ Acknowledgment | ☐ Driver's License | | |
| ☐ Other: | ☐ Other: | | |

| | | |
|---|---|---|
| Witness Full Name: | Phone Number: | |
| Email Address: | Witness Signature: | Thumbprint: |
| Address: | | |
| Document Type: | Date/Time Notarized: | Document Date: | |
| Comments: | | | |

## NOTARY LOG

| | | |
|---|---|---|
| Full Name | Phone Number: | Record Number: **212** |
| Email Address: | Signer's Signature: | $ Amount charged: |
| Address: | | Method of Payment: |
| | Gas & Mileage: | ☐ Cash  ☐ Credit  ☐ Check |
| Notary Service(s) Provided: | Identification: | ID Number: |
| ☐ Jurat | ☐ ID Card  ☐ Credible Witness | Issued By: |
| ☐ Oath/Affirmations | ☐ Passport  ☐ Known Personally | Date Issued: | Expiration Date: |
| ☐ Acknowledgment | ☐ Driver's License | | |
| ☐ Other: | ☐ Other: | | |

| | | |
|---|---|---|
| Witness Full Name: | Phone Number: | |
| Email Address: | Witness Signature: | Thumbprint: |
| Address: | | |
| Document Type: | Date/Time Notarized: | Document Date: | |
| Comments: | | | |

## NOTARY LOG

| Full Name | Phone Number: | Record Number: **213** |
|---|---|---|
| Email Address: | Signer's Signature: | $ Amount charged: |
| Address: | | Method of Payment: |
| | Gas & Mileage: | ☐ Cash   ☐ Credit   ☐ Check |

| Notary Service(s) Provided: | Identification: | ID Number: |
|---|---|---|
| ☐ Jurat | ☐ ID Card   ☐ Credible Witness | Issued By: |
| ☐ Oath/Affirmations | ☐ Passport   ☐ Known Personally | Date Issued:   Expiration Date: |
| ☐ Acknowledgment | ☐ Driver's License | |
| ☐ Other: | ☐ Other: | |

| Witness Full Name: | Phone Number: | |
|---|---|---|
| Email Address: | Witness Signature: | Thumbprint: |
| Address: | | |

| Document Type: | Date/Time Notarized: | Document Date: |
|---|---|---|
| Comments: | | |

## NOTARY LOG

| Full Name | Phone Number: | Record Number: **214** |
|---|---|---|
| Email Address: | Signer's Signature: | $ Amount charged: |
| Address: | | Method of Payment: |
| | Gas & Mileage: | ☐ Cash   ☐ Credit   ☐ Check |

| Notary Service(s) Provided: | Identification: | ID Number: |
|---|---|---|
| ☐ Jurat | ☐ ID Card   ☐ Credible Witness | Issued By: |
| ☐ Oath/Affirmations | ☐ Passport   ☐ Known Personally | Date Issued:   Expiration Date: |
| ☐ Acknowledgment | ☐ Driver's License | |
| ☐ Other: | ☐ Other: | |

| Witness Full Name: | Phone Number: | |
|---|---|---|
| Email Address: | Witness Signature: | Thumbprint: |
| Address: | | |

| Document Type: | Date/Time Notarized: | Document Date: |
|---|---|---|
| Comments: | | |

## NOTARY LOG

| Full Name | Phone Number: | Record Number: **215** |
|---|---|---|
| Email Address: | Signer's Signature: | $ Amount charged: |
| Address: | | Method of Payment: |
| | Gas & Mileage: | ☐ Cash   ☐ Credit   ☐ Check |

| Notary Service(s) Provided: | Identification: | ID Number: |
|---|---|---|
| ☐ Jurat | ☐ ID Card   ☐ Credible Witness | Issued By: |
| ☐ Oath/Affirmations | ☐ Passport   ☐ Known Personally | Date Issued:   Expiration Date: |
| ☐ Acknowledgment | ☐ Driver's License | |
| ☐ Other: | ☐ Other: | |

| Witness Full Name: | Phone Number: | |
|---|---|---|
| Email Address: | Witness Signature: | Thumbprint: |
| Address: | | |

| Document Type: | Date/Time Notarized: | Document Date: |
|---|---|---|
| Comments: | | |

## NOTARY LOG

| Full Name | Phone Number: | Record Number: **216** |
|---|---|---|
| Email Address: | Signer's Signature: | $ Amount charged: |
| Address: | | Method of Payment: |
| | Gas & Mileage: | ☐ Cash   ☐ Credit   ☐ Check |

| Notary Service(s) Provided: | Identification: | ID Number: |
|---|---|---|
| ☐ Jurat | ☐ ID Card   ☐ Credible Witness | Issued By: |
| ☐ Oath/Affirmations | ☐ Passport   ☐ Known Personally | Date Issued:   Expiration Date: |
| ☐ Acknowledgment | ☐ Driver's License | |
| ☐ Other: | ☐ Other: | |

| Witness Full Name: | Phone Number: | |
|---|---|---|
| Email Address: | Witness Signature: | Thumbprint: |
| Address: | | |

| Document Type: | Date/Time Notarized: | Document Date: |
|---|---|---|
| Comments: | | |

# NOTARY LOG

| Full Name | Phone Number: | Record Number: **217** |
|---|---|---|
| Email Address: | Signer's Signature: | $ Amount charged: |
| Address: | | Method of Payment: |
| | Gas & Mileage: | ☐ Cash   ☐ Credit   ☐ Check |

| Notary Service(s) Provided: | Identification: | ID Number: |
|---|---|---|
| ☐ Jurat | ☐ ID Card   ☐ Credible Witness | Issued By: |
| ☐ Oath/Affirmations | ☐ Passport   ☐ Known Personally | Date Issued:   Expiration Date: |
| ☐ Acknowledgment | ☐ Driver's License | |
| ☐ Other: | ☐ Other: | |

| Witness Full Name: | Phone Number: | |
|---|---|---|
| Email Address: | Witness Signature: | Thumbprint: |
| Address: | | |

| Document Type: | Date/Time Notarized: | Document Date: |
|---|---|---|
| Comments: | | |

# NOTARY LOG

| Full Name | Phone Number: | Record Number: **218** |
|---|---|---|
| Email Address: | Signer's Signature: | $ Amount charged: |
| Address: | | Method of Payment: |
| | Gas & Mileage: | ☐ Cash   ☐ Credit   ☐ Check |

| Notary Service(s) Provided: | Identification: | ID Number: |
|---|---|---|
| ☐ Jurat | ☐ ID Card   ☐ Credible Witness | Issued By: |
| ☐ Oath/Affirmations | ☐ Passport   ☐ Known Personally | Date Issued:   Expiration Date: |
| ☐ Acknowledgment | ☐ Driver's License | |
| ☐ Other: | ☐ Other: | |

| Witness Full Name: | Phone Number: | |
|---|---|---|
| Email Address: | Witness Signature: | Thumbprint: |
| Address: | | |

| Document Type: | Date/Time Notarized: | Document Date: |
|---|---|---|
| Comments: | | |

## NOTARY LOG

| Full Name | Phone Number: | Record Number: **219** |
|---|---|---|
| Email Address: | Signer's Signature: | $ Amount charged: |
| Address: | | Method of Payment: |
| | Gas & Mileage: | ☐ Cash   ☐ Credit   ☐ Check |

| Notary Service(s) Provided: | Identification: | ID Number: |
|---|---|---|
| ☐ Jurat | ☐ ID Card   ☐ Credible Witness | Issued By: |
| ☐ Oath/Affirmations | ☐ Passport   ☐ Known Personally | Date Issued:   Expiration Date: |
| ☐ Acknowledgment | ☐ Driver's License | |
| ☐ Other: | ☐ Other: | |

Witness Full Name:   Phone Number:

| Email Address: | Witness Signature: | Thumbprint: |
|---|---|---|
| Address: | | |

| Document Type: | Date/Time Notarized: | Document Date: |
|---|---|---|

Comments:

---

## NOTARY LOG

| Full Name | Phone Number: | Record Number: **220** |
|---|---|---|
| Email Address: | Signer's Signature: | $ Amount charged: |
| Address: | | Method of Payment: |
| | Gas & Mileage: | ☐ Cash   ☐ Credit   ☐ Check |

| Notary Service(s) Provided: | Identification: | ID Number: |
|---|---|---|
| ☐ Jurat | ☐ ID Card   ☐ Credible Witness | Issued By: |
| ☐ Oath/Affirmations | ☐ Passport   ☐ Known Personally | Date Issued:   Expiration Date: |
| ☐ Acknowledgment | ☐ Driver's License | |
| ☐ Other: | ☐ Other: | |

Witness Full Name:   Phone Number:

| Email Address: | Witness Signature: | Thumbprint: |
|---|---|---|
| Address: | | |

| Document Type: | Date/Time Notarized: | Document Date: |
|---|---|---|

Comments:

## NOTARY LOG

| Full Name | Phone Number: | Record Number: **221** |
|---|---|---|
| Email Address: | Signer's Signature: | $ Amount charged: |
| Address: | | Method of Payment: |
| | Gas & Mileage: | ☐ Cash  ☐ Credit  ☐ Check |

| Notary Service(s) Provided: | Identification: | ID Number: |
|---|---|---|
| ☐ Jurat | ☐ ID Card  ☐ Credible Witness | Issued By: |
| ☐ Oath/Affirmations | ☐ Passport  ☐ Known Personally | Date Issued:  Expiration Date: |
| ☐ Acknowledgment | ☐ Driver's License | |
| ☐ Other: | ☐ Other: | |

| Witness Full Name: | Phone Number: | |
|---|---|---|
| Email Address: | Witness Signature: | Thumbprint: |
| Address: | | |

| Document Type: | Date/Time Notarized: | Document Date: |
|---|---|---|

Comments:

---

## NOTARY LOG

| Full Name | Phone Number: | Record Number: **222** |
|---|---|---|
| Email Address: | Signer's Signature: | $ Amount charged: |
| Address: | | Method of Payment: |
| | Gas & Mileage: | ☐ Cash  ☐ Credit  ☐ Check |

| Notary Service(s) Provided: | Identification: | ID Number: |
|---|---|---|
| ☐ Jurat | ☐ ID Card  ☐ Credible Witness | Issued By: |
| ☐ Oath/Affirmations | ☐ Passport  ☐ Known Personally | Date Issued:  Expiration Date: |
| ☐ Acknowledgment | ☐ Driver's License | |
| ☐ Other: | ☐ Other: | |

| Witness Full Name: | Phone Number: | |
|---|---|---|
| Email Address: | Witness Signature: | Thumbprint: |
| Address: | | |

| Document Type: | Date/Time Notarized: | Document Date: |
|---|---|---|

Comments:

## NOTARY LOG

| | | |
|---|---|---|
| Full Name | Phone Number: | Record Number: **223** |
| Email Address: | Signer's Signature: | $ Amount charged: |
| Address: | | Method of Payment: |
| | Gas & Mileage: | ☐ Cash  ☐ Credit  ☐ Check |

Notary Service(s) Provided:  |  Identification:  |  ID Number:
☐ Jurat  |  ☐ ID Card   ☐ Credible Witness  |  Issued By:
☐ Oath/Affirmations  |  ☐ Passport   ☐ Known Personally  |  Date Issued:   Expiration Date:
☐ Acknowledgment  |  ☐ Driver's License
☐ Other:  |  ☐ Other:

Witness Full Name:  |  Phone Number:
Email Address:  |  Witness Signature:  |  Thumbprint:
Address:

Document Type:  |  Date/Time Notarized:  |  Document Date:
Comments:

---

## NOTARY LOG

| | | |
|---|---|---|
| Full Name | Phone Number: | Record Number: **224** |
| Email Address: | Signer's Signature: | $ Amount charged: |
| Address: | | Method of Payment: |
| | Gas & Mileage: | ☐ Cash  ☐ Credit  ☐ Check |

Notary Service(s) Provided:  |  Identification:  |  ID Number:
☐ Jurat  |  ☐ ID Card   ☐ Credible Witness  |  Issued By:
☐ Oath/Affirmations  |  ☐ Passport   ☐ Known Personally  |  Date Issued:   Expiration Date:
☐ Acknowledgment  |  ☐ Driver's License
☐ Other:  |  ☐ Other:

Witness Full Name:  |  Phone Number:
Email Address:  |  Witness Signature:  |  Thumbprint:
Address:

Document Type:  |  Date/Time Notarized:  |  Document Date:
Comments:

## NOTARY LOG

| Full Name | Phone Number: | Record Number: **225** |
|---|---|---|
| Email Address: | Signer's Signature: | $ Amount charged: |
| Address: | | Method of Payment: |
| | Gas & Mileage: | ☐ Cash   ☐ Credit   ☐ Check |

| Notary Service(s) Provided: | Identification: | ID Number: |
|---|---|---|
| ☐ Jurat | ☐ ID Card   ☐ Credible Witness | Issued By: |
| ☐ Oath/Affirmations | ☐ Passport   ☐ Known Personally | Date Issued:   Expiration Date: |
| ☐ Acknowledgment | ☐ Driver's License | |
| ☐ Other: | ☐ Other: | |

| Witness Full Name: | Phone Number: | |
|---|---|---|
| Email Address: | Witness Signature: | Thumbprint: |
| Address: | | |

| Document Type: | Date/Time Notarized: | Document Date: | |
|---|---|---|---|
| Comments: | | | |

## NOTARY LOG

| Full Name | Phone Number: | Record Number: **226** |
|---|---|---|
| Email Address: | Signer's Signature: | $ Amount charged: |
| Address: | | Method of Payment: |
| | Gas & Mileage: | ☐ Cash   ☐ Credit   ☐ Check |

| Notary Service(s) Provided: | Identification: | ID Number: |
|---|---|---|
| ☐ Jurat | ☐ ID Card   ☐ Credible Witness | Issued By: |
| ☐ Oath/Affirmations | ☐ Passport   ☐ Known Personally | Date Issued:   Expiration Date: |
| ☐ Acknowledgment | ☐ Driver's License | |
| ☐ Other: | ☐ Other: | |

| Witness Full Name: | Phone Number: | |
|---|---|---|
| Email Address: | Witness Signature: | Thumbprint: |
| Address: | | |

| Document Type: | Date/Time Notarized: | Document Date: | |
|---|---|---|---|
| Comments: | | | |

## NOTARY LOG

| Full Name | Phone Number: | Record Number: **227** |
|---|---|---|
| Email Address: | Signer's Signature: | $ Amount charged: |
| Address: | | Method of Payment: |
| | Gas & Mileage: | ☐ Cash  ☐ Credit  ☐ Check |

| Notary Service(s) Provided: | Identification: | ID Number: |
|---|---|---|
| ☐ Jurat | ☐ ID Card  ☐ Credible Witness | Issued By: |
| ☐ Oath/Affirmations | ☐ Passport  ☐ Known Personally | Date Issued:  Expiration Date: |
| ☐ Acknowledgment | ☐ Driver's License | |
| ☐ Other: | ☐ Other: | |

| Witness Full Name: | Phone Number: | |
|---|---|---|
| Email Address: | Witness Signature: | Thumbprint: |
| Address: | | |

| Document Type: | Date/Time Notarized: | Document Date: |
|---|---|---|

Comments:

---

## NOTARY LOG

| Full Name | Phone Number: | Record Number: **228** |
|---|---|---|
| Email Address: | Signer's Signature: | $ Amount charged: |
| Address: | | Method of Payment: |
| | Gas & Mileage: | ☐ Cash  ☐ Credit  ☐ Check |

| Notary Service(s) Provided: | Identification: | ID Number: |
|---|---|---|
| ☐ Jurat | ☐ ID Card  ☐ Credible Witness | Issued By: |
| ☐ Oath/Affirmations | ☐ Passport  ☐ Known Personally | Date Issued:  Expiration Date: |
| ☐ Acknowledgment | ☐ Driver's License | |
| ☐ Other: | ☐ Other: | |

| Witness Full Name: | Phone Number: | |
|---|---|---|
| Email Address: | Witness Signature: | Thumbprint: |
| Address: | | |

| Document Type: | Date/Time Notarized: | Document Date: |
|---|---|---|

Comments:

## NOTARY LOG

| Full Name | Phone Number: | Record Number: **229** |
|---|---|---|
| Email Address: | Signer's Signature: | $ Amount charged: |
| Address: | | Method of Payment: |
| | Gas & Mileage: | ☐ Cash ☐ Credit ☐ Check |

| Notary Service(s) Provided: | Identification: | ID Number: |
|---|---|---|
| ☐ Jurat | ☐ ID Card ☐ Credible Witness | Issued By: |
| ☐ Oath/Affirmations | ☐ Passport ☐ Known Personally | Date Issued: / Expiration Date: |
| ☐ Acknowledgment | ☐ Driver's License | |
| ☐ Other: | ☐ Other: | |

| Witness Full Name: | Phone Number: | |
|---|---|---|
| Email Address: | Witness Signature: | Thumbprint: |
| Address: | | |

| Document Type: | Date/Time Notarized: | Document Date: |
|---|---|---|

Comments:

---

## NOTARY LOG

| Full Name | Phone Number: | Record Number: **230** |
|---|---|---|
| Email Address: | Signer's Signature: | $ Amount charged: |
| Address: | | Method of Payment: |
| | Gas & Mileage: | ☐ Cash ☐ Credit ☐ Check |

| Notary Service(s) Provided: | Identification: | ID Number: |
|---|---|---|
| ☐ Jurat | ☐ ID Card ☐ Credible Witness | Issued By: |
| ☐ Oath/Affirmations | ☐ Passport ☐ Known Personally | Date Issued: / Expiration Date: |
| ☐ Acknowledgment | ☐ Driver's License | |
| ☐ Other: | ☐ Other: | |

| Witness Full Name: | Phone Number: | |
|---|---|---|
| Email Address: | Witness Signature: | Thumbprint: |
| Address: | | |

| Document Type: | Date/Time Notarized: | Document Date: |
|---|---|---|

Comments:

## NOTARY LOG

| | | |
|---|---|---|
| Full Name | Phone Number: | Record Number: **231** |
| Email Address: | Signer's Signature: | $ Amount charged: |
| Address: | | Method of Payment: |
| | Gas & Mileage: | ☐ Cash ☐ Credit ☐ Check |
| Notary Service(s) Provided: | Identification: | ID Number: |
| ☐ Jurat | ☐ ID Card ☐ Credible Witness | Issued By: |
| ☐ Oath/Affirmations | ☐ Passport ☐ Known Personally | Date Issued: | Expiration Date: |
| ☐ Acknowledgment | ☐ Driver's License | |
| ☐ Other: | ☐ Other: | |

| | | |
|---|---|---|
| Witness Full Name: | Phone Number: | |
| Email Address: | Witness Signature: | Thumbprint: |
| Address: | | |
| Document Type: | Date/Time Notarized: | Document Date: |
| Comments: | | |

## NOTARY LOG

| | | |
|---|---|---|
| Full Name | Phone Number: | Record Number: **232** |
| Email Address: | Signer's Signature: | $ Amount charged: |
| Address: | | Method of Payment: |
| | Gas & Mileage: | ☐ Cash ☐ Credit ☐ Check |
| Notary Service(s) Provided: | Identification: | ID Number: |
| ☐ Jurat | ☐ ID Card ☐ Credible Witness | Issued By: |
| ☐ Oath/Affirmations | ☐ Passport ☐ Known Personally | Date Issued: | Expiration Date: |
| ☐ Acknowledgment | ☐ Driver's License | |
| ☐ Other: | ☐ Other: | |

| | | |
|---|---|---|
| Witness Full Name: | Phone Number: | |
| Email Address: | Witness Signature: | Thumbprint: |
| Address: | | |
| Document Type: | Date/Time Notarized: | Document Date: |
| Comments: | | |

Made in the USA
Coppell, TX
25 November 2021